WOMEN, DIVORCE, AND MONEY

WOMEN, DIVORCE, AND MONEY

MARY ROGERS

McGRAW-HILL BOOK COMPANY

New York *St. Louis* *San Francisco*
Toronto *Hamburg* *Mexico*

1 2 3 4 5 6 7 8 9 B P B P 8 7 6 5 4 3 2 1

LIBRARY OF CONGRESS CATALOGING IN PUBLICATION DATA

Rogers, Mary, 1916–
Women, divorce, and money.
Includes index.
1. Divorcees—United States—Life skills guides.
I. Title.
HQ834.R63   306.8'9   80-28648
ISBN 0-07-053496-9

Book design by Christine Aulicino.

CONTENTS

INTRODUCTION

DIVORCE LAWS IN THIS COUNTRY today are a mess. Attorneys know it, judges know it, lawmakers know it—and divorcing wives and husbands know it best of all.

Each state differs in its provision for the divorced wife and in its attitudes about her. Each county of each state is apt to be a little different, too. And the judge you get today may hand down a very different court order from the one you might have received in that same town from a different judge yesterday or tomorrow, or at a different time of day. The judgments, however sincere and knowledgeable, will necessarily haunt the man, the woman, and the children involved for the rest of their lives.

Essentially, these are *financial decisions*. In more and more states, divorce has come to be a "no-fault" situation as far as the law is concerned. Grievances, in general, are no longer being heard. Obviously there is much merit in this. Anger and envy are being declared irrelevant. Revenge is not recognized in most states as a proper motive in family law, and we can be glad of this. Yet there are a great many women in this country today who bartered their independence long ago for the sort of financial security that was once guaranteed on moral grounds. If the woman "behaved" (or did not get caught "misbehaving"), she was entitled to support as a financially valuable asset: a housewife, a manager, a mother of the tribe. The law recognized her worth as such.

Under the new rules, women who have never worked outside the home are suddenly being dumped on the labor market in ever-increasing numbers without skills that would enable them to find employment, in a time of economic uncertainty and in a period that still favors males over females at a pay-scale ratio of ten to six. Many of these women's younger sisters have assumed from the beginning that they would have to develop abilities marketable outside the home. For the young, career-minded woman of the New Age the situation may not be so desperate as it is for women caught between cultures in this way; however, she may have young children who need a great deal of her time and energy, particularly during the time of emotional upheaval following divorce, and she may be unable to re-enter the job market immediately.

There are additional psychological problems for the middle-aged woman, suddenly divorced, who has always been dependent upon a man's income. She was taught the dignity and propriety of private life. As a woman, she knew that she ought to be modest, retiring, deferential, unacquainted with the hard realities of financial and political life. She was to develop only her nurturing and artistic talents. She was to be a good cook, a good laundress, a good cleaning woman. In return for this, and for her unpaid—often unacknowledged—work as mother and teacher of the next generation, she would be protected by her male partner in marriage, in widowhood, or in divorce.

Now, with nearly 50 percent of marriages ending

in divorce (and an increasing percentage in marriages of over twenty years) this woman's identity is stripped from her along with her financial base. She is exposed to the public glare, very often during her own midlife crisis, and told that she is incompetent if she cannot suddenly manage to come up with a means of supporting herself—and very often supporting the children of the marriage as well. Very few states award alimony. Very few husbands pay child support even when it is awarded by the court.

Younger women, looking at their options, are deciding in great numbers not to get married at all. If they plan to educate their children, they are thinking very, very carefully before having any.

It is a bad situation, yes—a real, twenty-carat mess. But just because the situation is a mess doesn't mean that you, a woman getting a divorce, need to be a mess.

I have counseled a great many women throughout the divorce process and have helped them make new lives for themselves. I am well aware of the discouraging statistics and the horror stories—the great numbers of "new poor" among middle-class women who are now living a marginal existence at best because of divorce. *This needn't happen to you.*

This book takes you step by step through the process of divorce and into a new life of independence and self-respect. My position on the whole matter is a tough one. You will get plenty of understanding from me, but you may not get as much sympathy as you think you need. You need something more than sympathy—you need real assistance, and that begins with the development of a new point of view: *Take a look at yourself, lady, and admit that we have been sold a bill of goods.*

I'll bet you believed it too: that little cottage with the white picket fence around it; the husband and the wife who loved each other so dearly all their days. The single daughter, the 2.5 sons, the dog, the cat, the kitchen floor without yellow stain buildup, the shirts coming out of the wash without ring around the collar. Growing old together, he putters in his workshop and goes fishing; she is in the kitchen with the grandchildren baking apple pies. They still love each other, and there is plenty of money coming from somewhere.

This is Pollyanna stuff. Begin your divorce by putting it on the junk heap and forgetting it. Most women in this world have always worked two jobs. I kept house in the 1930s with a broom, a copper boiler to do the clothes in, and a scrub board. Until very recent years in American history the middle class had no money in the savings bank. Women worked in the fields driving the tractor and cooking meals for farmhands or lived over the store and helped to tend it in the daytime while keeping house without any modern appliances. The upper classes had hired help, but the upper-class housewife worked as hard as the kitchen girl who had just gotten off the boat.

Until recently, when there was a divorce, the man just walked away. The woman organized. *She took control.* She parceled out the jobs to be done among the children and saw to it that they cooperated. She was the adult in the situation. She rolled up her sleeves and saw to it that the family survived. Don't forget that in those days there was no such thing as retirement. Probably you didn't grow old—you died instead. There weren't so many divorces in those days because people had a chance to change partners every few years on account of early deaths, particularly among women in childbirth. The occasional woman outlived as many as four or five husbands. It was not at all unusual for a man to marry and bury that many wives.

If you did live to be very old and quite unemployable, you *might* be cared for by your family if you were lucky. There was no protection for females written into the law. If you think that the law has ever guaranteed you the kind of existence you see in the television ads or in magazines like *Good Housekeeping,* lady, you are dreaming. And if you have bought that dream, you have forgotten about the real meaning of being a woman. You have forgotten that women, for centuries on end, have been the ones quietly seeing to it that the human race survives. If you are going to do that, you have got to survive yourself.

So, when you think about divorce, begin by taking a very practical look at the institution of marriage to begin with. If you have married for love, then you are a part of a very small minority in human history. Historically, the marriages of the rich and powerful have been planned to combine forces for political and financial reasons. The poor have married to escape family drudgery or starvation. Women everywhere have been seen as sources of free labor and physical carriers of the next generation. Men made the laws—and the laws were made, quite naturally, to protect men.

We're in a time of change now, and that change is frightening to women who weren't prepared for it. But the point of the change is that women are at last being recognized as *equal financial partners.* New laws recognizing the responsibility of women to work are also tending to acknowledge women's equal rights to the ownership of community property. Too often, it is true, in middle-class, middle-age divorces today we see the husband walking away with the greatest asset the marriage has—his own earning power. If he has been improvident there may be nothing much left to divide except the family home (and the mortgage on that) and a pile of debts. *But even the woman left in this situation can make it.*

Divorce hurts. I know it hurts. But all growth is painful. There are ways to help. I want to help you make this a time of personal and financial recovery that you will look back on with satisfaction and pride.

I want the women who read this book to go into court, wherever they are, prepared to fight for their rights as *equal financial partners in the marriage.* I want them to go prepared with a plan for their own future that will give them the best possible chance of obtaining *court-ordered temporary support* while they develop for themselves an independent, productive, and gratifying style of existence. I want women to develop the self-respect that no financially dependent individual, male or female, can possibly have in the twentieth century if that woman or that man is healthy, capable, and adult. If some battles like this are lost, then others will be won when more and more women enter the legal forum with heads held high and cool intelligence at work.

It is time for us now to consider divorce, however painful and frightening, not as the ultimate disaster but as a challenge. Whatever the cause for your divorce, read this book in a spirit of hope. There *is* hope, you know. This ending can be the best new beginning you ever had. The past is past. Put it away—and turn the page

WOMEN, DIVORCE, AND MONEY

Chapter 1

WHERE AM I?

PANIC IS THE AVERAGE WOMAN'S first response to the realization that she is about to be divorced. She may know perfectly well that her present life is an emotional disaster area, but the future is going to look even more terrifying to her right now. *Why? What is the real basis for her fear? Is there anything we can do about it?*

You bet there is. There is plenty we can do about it. We are dealing here with fear of the unknown. If you are getting a divorce—particularly if you have been married for a number of years—you are facing the fact that you have been dependent on another person for quite some time. "Dependent" in this situation has a dollar sign next to it. It is only natural for you to fear a life for yourself, and perhaps for your children too, without adequate funds. The issue of money in divorce is almost always the big one. It tends to distort and color every other issue, and it causes no end of trouble for everyone involved.

You are afraid of the future because it looks like a big question mark from here. But with the help you need, you can take charge of it—you can take charge of yourself, beginning here and now. *You have the power to turn your life around so that this experience can be an opportunity instead of a disaster.* You can regroup your forces, reorganize your priorities, and plan a new life that will give you what you really want. Impossible? That word doesn't belong in your vocabulary now.

It's going to be tricky, because you are going to have to prepare for temporary survival (Survival: Stage One) in the midst of your worst emotional upset. Let's start coping with this panic of yours before you make a single move. Put it on a shelf somewhere in a brown bag and label it *panic.* You don't need it now. Fear causes wild, angry reactions. It tempts you to hateful, hurtful behavior in the foolish search for revenge. If you are aware that the fury you are feeling is based on fear, you will be way ahead of the game. You'll prevent yourself from doing the kind of thing you'll surely live to regret.

Fear needs to be dealt with under a bright light, with a clear head. It helps if you have a companion to take a look at it with you, and this book is designed to be your companion while you calmly organize your divorce *as a financial transaction.* My purpose here is to see that you run your life as a confident, grown-up person instead of letting your emotions take over at a crucial moment like this.

Let me tell you, first and foremost, what *not* to do. A woman I will call Barbara is a good case in point. Barbara's husband came home one night and announced that he was leaving her. He had already taken an apartment, he said, and would be moving his things out the following day. Understandably, Barbara went into shock. She had known that their marriage was far from perfect, but she had been telling herself that all marriages get into this condition after fifteen years or so. She had assumed that things would improve in time—and she had been wrong.

The die was cast. John said he had "filed," but she was not quite sure what that meant. Did she have to file too? What was supposed to happen next? Barbara called a friend and asked for help. Together they looked in the yellow pages of the telephone book, and she called the first name on a list of attorneys. She made an immediate appointment, still not understanding what was going on.

Barbara was running to an authority figure at this point because she was terrified and she believed down deep that he would somehow make things come out right for her. But she was not at all prepared for a meeting with this high-powered, expensive professional. He was a busy man, and she had not begun to deal with her emotions. None of her financial records was in order. Too bad! Until she had things a great deal better organized than this, the most the attorney could do was to hold her hand and supply Kleenex at $75 an hour. What a waste! *I want you to do things differently.*

Don't Sell Yourself down the River

The transaction of divorce is probably the most important financial event that will occur in a woman's life. You wouldn't run downtown in a hysterical state to buy or sell something as important as a car, a house, or a piece of property without any of the facts in hand. Why do this in relation to something far more important—your own future financial security and well-being?

Do your crying at home, not in your attorney's office. You are hiring this person to advise you on the law, not to put Band-aids on your gaping emotional wounds. Cry with your friends, if necessary, free of charge. Then dry your eyes and begin looking long and hard at dollars and cents.

You are going to have to come to a complete understanding of your financial situation as it has been, and as it is likely to be in future years. It's a big order and you won't be able to do it all in a day or a week. But in order to protect yourself during Survival: Stage One, you are going to have to get going right now with some intelligent research and some plain, ordinary hard work.

"But I don't know anything about money," you may say. Or "I have never been good with figures." Or "My husband makes all the financial decisions" or "I haven't time" or "I could never. . . ." Well, that's rubbish.

Women have been programmed long enough to believe that money and its management are the privilege only of a male. Earlier in our country's history wives and widows managed all sorts of trading, shipping, and other business ventures. They supervised enormous estates in the temporary or permanent absence of their men, and most of them did a splendid job of it. The idea that women can't function as well as men in making financial decisions is absolute nonsense, and it has got to go. Women are quite capable of taking this sort of responsibility. They can make plans that reflect their own needs, their own abilities, and their own goals. If you will get rid of this automatic attitude of helplessness and hopelessness, you can do it too.

First Things First

I am going to tell you in great detail how to prepare yourself *before* you run in for that first visit to an attorney. But first, you need to understand why this is such an important thing for you to do. It's not just a matter of saving the price of an irrelevant visit. You must have your facts and your ideas in order before you walk into that office, because you are going to assert yourself in this important transaction. You are going to be treated here as a thinking individual. You are not going to sit back like a ninny and let your future be decided by "experts" who don't even know you and often couldn't care less. If you get ready now, you won't wish later that you had understood what the others were talking about. There may be options for you that no one but yourself will ever think to mention. If you let yourself be perceived as a person incapable of making decisions, soon you won't be presented with any decisions to make.

In this book we will go about preparing your case just as thoroughly and professionally as possible. *Then* you will be ready to hire specialists to assist you, and you will be able to command their respect. You will communicate with them on an equal basis, and you will discover that you have choices. You will weigh these choices for your own benefit, and you will not be in the position of accepting blindly any suggestions for settlement made by others.

How to Know When

Very often the finances of divorce begin long before the idea of separation enters the picture. This is a good time for you to look back at your marriage and come to a better understanding of the overall patterns that have been governing your financial life. I am not suggesting that every woman who picks up this book will be some innocent victim whose husband of many years has just walked out and left her flat. Many of you have been struggling with the idea of divorce for years, and have decided to go for it on your own. Money has been a real part of the problem in many of your marriages.

Margy, for example, had a husband who was financially irresponsible over a long period of time during which she worked hard to keep the marriage together. His drinking was ruining their lives in more ways than one, and they were heavily in debt. Margy kept thinking that things would change for the better, but they never did. Toward the end she knew Sam was thinking of borrowing again on the home that was the very last thing of value they had. She decided that she had no future at all unless she obtained a divorce. If she made a move now, at least they could share the remaining value of the house and, little as that was, it would help to give her a new start in life. She drew up detailed statements of the present financial situation, took her courage in her hands, and went to an attorney.

Claire found that her emotional and her financial development were both halted, simply stopped cold, by the circumstances of her marriage. She had been the certifiably correct Wife and Mother year after year, according to her favorite sources in *Good Housekeeping* and *The Ladies' Home Journal.* At least her children were out of the nest and she began to realize that it was time for her to develop a Self.

Claire had done volunteer work all through the mothering years, and she now wanted a paid job with a future in it. She looked around, had a good offer, and then the axe fell. *No wife of mine will ever work,* her husband Jim announced. There was absolutely no way she could convince him that she would not abandon him, that she was quite capable of caring beautifully for their home and holding down a rewarding job at the same time. Months passed and her frustration grew. Claire was only forty-two years old and could not bear to think that she would spend the rest of her life under this kind of ownership. Jim was a salesman, away from home a great deal, so it was absentee ownership at that. Claire was a gutsy gal. She walked away from the home she had created and filed for divorce.

Both these women prepared themselves intelligently for the future, and both are now fully independent, successful human beings. How did they do it? First of all, they took the responsibility for learning something about the divorce laws in their own states, so that they would know what they were getting into. You should put a call to your state commission on the status of women at the very top of your own list. You'll be asking for information about your local divorce laws, and the commission should be able to direct you to the right source. Read the rules pertaining to your own temporary support, division of property, custody and support of children, and guidelines for settlement. Get to know in detail the steps that are taken in your state to end a marriage and you will save yourself a great deal of time, money, and energy.

Now is the time to set aside any notions you may have about either partner getting "cleaned out" by a divorce. It is not in the interests of your state—any state—to see either party in a divorce end up on welfare. Money that actually exists in the situation can rarely be hidden from the eyes of a good forensic accountant who knows where to hunt. It is a waste of energy for either partner to play games of this sort. Don't be unnecessarily afraid of it and don't try anything like it yourself: you need your energy for better things. Inform yourself, instead, about the realistic possibilities that lie ahead of you.

Facing It

Now it is time for you to find out exactly how much it costs you to live. This step isn't going to be much fun, but it is an important part of your campaign. You are collecting the data you are going to need for your attorney, and at the same time you are building the self-knowledge that will help you to become a more responsible, self-confident person in days to come. Remember, this is a big turning point. What you do with paper and pencil right now may actually determine whether you will end your days helpless and poor or whether you will go on from here to make a good life for yourself.

Gather all of your canceled checks and/or check records for the past year and make a careful study of them. "Oh, no!" you may say. "Is this really necessary?" Yes, it is. We have to have a complete record of your ordinary spending before we can begin to know what your basic budget ought to look like. Gone is the day when you accepted a check from your husband, or found a deposit in your account, and began to pay the bills without much thought one way or another. You are going to be aware of what you are doing from now on, and you are going to know exactly why you are doing it.

Sort your checks out by number and then begin to make some headings on a piece of paper, either by hand or with a typewriter, something like this:

Ck #	Date	Name	Amt	Household	Childr.	Special
23	1/1	Electric	42.54	42.54		
24	1/2	Cash	50.00	50.00		
25	1/2	Mortgage	451.00	451.00		
26	1/4	Shoes	22.10			22.10

You may arrange your various categories any way you wish as long as they are clear and convenient to work with. The idea is to find out what you are used to spending where and what the totals of the different categories are.

If you have children, their expenses should be recorded separately at this time. Medical expenses should also be kept separate. You may need support from a family counselor, a mental health clinic, or private services during this period of trauma and uncertainty.

There may also be extra costs on behalf of the children simply because the family as a whole is in crisis.

Under "Special" list expenses that occur once or twice a year, such as taxes, vacations, school expenses, insurance premiums. We will discuss these departments in depth in the following chapters. We will also show you in detail exactly what kind of information you are really gathering by this simple device of lining up your checks.

"But this is so much work!" some women say to me. It's not; it's very simple. It is just getting yourself started on it that is a trial. Many of us don't *want* to see clearly what has been happening in our checkbooks. Some money, very likely, has been foolishly wasted. Some irresponsible spending has been taking place. Well, so be it. Every one of us has done some stupid spending over the years. When you have to look at it this way, you have a chance to take another look at it and think it over. This in turn will help you not to make the same error again.

Some of the items you list won't give you a hint of what they bought for you. Are you finding a great many checks made out to Cash? Do you know what these were spent on? If you are in doubt, I have a suggestion for you. Next time around, place that money in a special pocketbook and ask for a receipt for each and every purchase that you make. Keep the receipts in the same place, and at the end of the month you will know exactly where your money went.

This is a good time to ask yourself "Is this cash going for *little spending?*" Many years ago a wise adviser of mine asked me to write down everything I spent, and I found that even in those days when we had a minimum income I was spending a lot of what I came to call *little money.* My own receipts showed me that I had rarely bought anything of real value, and I made up my mind that I would never again buy something that "only cost 29¢." That amount became symbolic for me of anything cheap that wouldn't work, wasn't beautiful, would surely be broken soon, and (if it was food) probably didn't even taste good. From that time on, I have held back on little spending—that cheap meal because I was too tired to cook or forgot my lunch, that impulse item cunningly placed beside the cash register. If I held back on little spending, I knew I was going to be able to spend big someday. I decided that was going to be more fun—and I was right.

What about those checks written for credit-card expenses? They don't serve to remind you of what you actually bought either. From now on, make up your mind that you are going to break down the amounts and make a note of individual items in your checkbook, so you will know what these were all about. I do a great deal of writing in my own checkbook, and I can tell you that it is very helpful. Question: Are you paying any interest for your use of the credit-card system? Did you know that interest can go as high as *30 percent,* depending on how it is computed? Don't let this happen to you! We are going to get control of these hidden expenses of yours so that you can live well from now on while spending less.

If you are like many of the women I have worked with, you are going to show some resistance to all this. However, I am going to insist that you have a realistic budget to present *before* you [file for divorce]. You have a case to make and you will have to substantiate your items; you can't just take them out of the air. More important, you need to know exactly the amounts of your fixed expenses because you are going to be responsible for yourself from now on. Basic food costs, mortgage payments or rent, utilities, insurance, taxes—all these must be listed carefully so that we will know the truth about your spending habits.

Of course you may find that you have a very pleasant surprise. You may look at these items and say "Hey, I'm really doing a very fine job!" So much the better. It is good to see it on a piece of paper, isn't it? Once you know how easy this is, you may want to do this for yourself, after your divorce, quarterly or at least twice a year. It will help you make decisions about your future spending. For example, you may want to forgo some other expense in order to buy tickets for entertainment, or you may find that you have developing goals about your children's future. This simple recording device will help you immeasurably in cutting down on frivolous spending. It will help you (if necessary) to ignore some of the neighborhood patterns around you. You don't have to follow the crowd. You're in charge of your own life now.

What if you don't know the total picture of your family spending? Perhaps a lot of the bills have been paid as a matter of course by your husband. He may keep his records in his office, and you may never have had a look at them. If his secretary knows more about your family finances than you do, this must change. The items he is paying for now are all a part of your total spending record. If he has been taking care of items such as the mortgage and the insurance, you need to know what these costs are—and you have a right to know.

You can't get an answer about them directly from your husband? Then you will have to do some investigating on your own. Who loaned you the money to buy your house? It could be a bank, or a savings and loan association. You are probably a co-owner, and your signature may well be on the application and the note. We will go into detail about real estate in a later chapter, but meantime ask some questions and begin to fill in as many of the blank spaces as you can yourself.

Figure out what it costs you each month for transportation, for shelter, for food, for all the basics in your life, and make lists now of the totals for all your columns. Include in this figuring a clear list of all loans you are now paying, and how much the charges are. Do you have a realistic plan for paying them off? Make a note of it. You are now looking at a clear picture of where your money has been going and of what choices you have made about the use of it in the past.

You've begun to learn the most important lesson I can teach you, too, when it comes to dealing with money. You've learned to take out a piece of paper and a pencil and *write it down.* From now on, don't ever try to struggle with money in the abstract. Don't ever think about money, or talk about money, or worry about money without a pencil in your hand. (Get a small pocket calculator if your arithmetic is fuzzy.) When it's there in front of you where you can see it, when you have got it put into some kind of order that makes sense, then you can begin to get control of it—and not until then. You'll be amazed how much grief this simple rule is going to spare you over the years to come.

Measuring Your Assets

Now that you have come through the first part of your preparation exercise with flying colors, do your best to gather a list of all your assets—of what the family owns. Remember, these lists can be amended if you find out more information at a later date, make a good beginning here and now. First, list the family home if you own one. If a couple has been married any length of time they usually do, for this has always been the American Dream, whether it is a house, a co-op apartment, a condominium, a mobile home, or a farm. We have been willing to go without luxuries to meet these monthly payments and now, with inflation biting into our spending power, we find even greater value in this investment we have made.

You will want the original purchase price of your

home as well as its present market value. If you can find the escrow paper showing all of the details of your purchase of your home, you have everything you need. This is the beginning of the financial history of your home. If this is not available, can you remember the real estate office where the transaction was begun? Its personnel can tell you which escrow office handled the details. Phone and ask them to search their records. Give the approximate date of purchase (probably a few days before you moved in), the address of the home, and your name. You may, of course, find among your old canceled checks a deposit or a check written which will give you the name of the escrow company. It helps if you know the name of the company that holds the mortgage, too. The present market value of your home could be found by asking a local realtor about the price that has been paid for homes like yours in your neighborhood.

Then list the unpaid amount of the mortgage (which can be found out by telephoning the bank or lending agency). Some lending agencies show the unpaid balance on your monthly statement. The difference between the unpaid balance and the market value is the amount of money you actually have, right now, in your home. Be sure, though, that there is not a second loan involved. Do you owe anyone money that you might have borrowed for the down payment? All of this has to be taken into consideration. Find out as much as you can about it now, and you will save yourself a great deal of trouble later on.

After your home, look next at the balances in your checking and savings accounts. If your husband has a separate account, this amount should also be listed. If you don't know how much or can't find this out, we will discuss how to get this information when we come to the matter of legal procedure.

Next, you need a list of all your other investments. Do you own any stocks or bonds? If so, list their current market value, which you can figure out by studying an issue of *The Wall Street Journal.* Some of your life insurance policies may have cash value. Look on the policy to find out. The front page of the policy will tell you how long it has been in force and the number of dollars in the face amount (the coverage). Find the schedule of cash or loan values in the policy, and by using the length of time and the number of thousands of dollars, determine the cash value. Your premium notice will tell you if you have ever borrowed any of these cash values.

Do you own any investment real estate, a lot, a vacation home? A tax-sheltered investment, a limited partnership? Does your husband contribute to a Keogh or an Individual Retirement Account? All of these are a part of the family's assets, and you must take them into account. If your husband is working for a corporation, he will probably have an ownership in his future pension plan or it may be listed as a profit-sharing plan. The value of these plans may be listed as family money. Does he have group insurance? A medical plan? Stock options? Write it down!

Don't forget to list the current value of your cars, trucks, boats, and any other vehicles, along with any unpaid balance there may be on these items. When you come to personal items, household furniture and appliances, it will be worth your while to make an inventory and estimate the current value. (Unless custom made or antique furniture is involved the estimate agreed upon by the couple is rarely disputed.) You see by now what you are trying to find: you want the very best possible picture of your family finances as a whole. *You worked for all this, whether or not you had a job outside the home. You must understand that clearly, when you look at the list that is beginning to take form in front of you.*

Two cautions now, before we are finished with this part of the job. First, most debts must be paid from your assets at the time of divorce. Second, if any of your investments have been given to either partner from an inheritance or by outright gift, a note should be made to this effect; these items may or may not be family money in the legal sense.

Making the IRS Work for You

No doubt you never thought of the Internal Revenue Service as a pal before, but it can perform a very valuable service for you at this point. You are going to need copies of the last two years (at least) of your federal and state income tax statements, and you may not find them lying around the house.

When I asked a client one time to obtain a copy of her income tax statement, she replied, "Oh, I *can't* get *them;* my husband's accountant would never give them to me!" I had to remind this woman that she had signed those tax statements, and that they were as much hers as they were her husband's. Sometimes you can get what you want very easily, simply by knowing your legal rights and applying them. But if you don't want to go to the family's source of tax information, you can always contact the nearest Internal Revenue Service office, giving your name and Social Security number. Indicate the years of filing you are looking for. They will send you copies of your forms for a small fee.

You will need these papers in order to document the kinds of statements you are going to make about your family income in the past, and they will also be an invaluable source for you and your attorney in tracking down items you might not otherwise have been aware of. If you have been afraid to look at them and to try to understand them before this, now is the time to take the plunge. *From now on, you are never going to sign a piece of paper again unless you thoroughly comprehend it.*

Getting It Together

One more step is necessary right away. Organize your information, I am not impressed with people who tell me about their four-drawer files filled with bits and scraps of papers from over the years. I don't want to see shoe boxes full of miscellaneous and irrelevant stuff. You must put your information together clearly and simply before it can be useful to you and your advisers. You have to know what you have and where it is, and it has to be updated as necessary.

Here's how to do it right. Buy a large loose-leaf binder and a dozen divider pages. (A good three-hole-punch device will be useful too.) This book is your Financial Notebook, and you are going to store all kinds of information very neatly in it. This notebook is going to be one of the essential pieces of equipment in your new life. Any time you go to an attorney, an accountant, or a broker from now on, you will have the facts and figures you need at your fingertips.

The first section will be a complete list of all your assets. Budget, if you like, can be the next. Following that could be divorce: a place to file all the necessary communications on this transaction, keeping these papers organized by date for easy access. This is where your three-hole punch will come in handy: letters to and from your attorney and other legal papers can be filed in place.

Insurance might be your next division. Policies can go here, except for life insurance policies which are sometimes difficult to replace. Take the information from your life insurance policies (having it duplicated on a copying machine is an easy way), place it in your book, and place the policies themselves in your safe deposit box.

Following this, you may want investments, then real estate or planning, and perhaps inheritance. Use the categories that apply to you. The purpose is to consolidate important material, and *it is important that you yourself do the work* so that you will know what is there and where to find everything. You can't do this overnight, of course. It will take time. But begin doing it now.

I have asked you to do a considerable amount of work, I know. If you say "I just can't!" I am sorry for you. You are really saying that you still want to be dependent, just because this is the role most women have been told they ought to take. Times are changing now. The woman of the 1980s is going to insist on being an equal partner in marriage, as in divorce. No one is going to take care of her future for her—and no one could do a better job than she can do for herself, when she takes charge of her own choices and takes responsibility for herself.

There is no such thing as a perfect divorce, any more than there is a perfect marriage. But remember that the purpose of the divorce court is to make fair and reasonable decisions. Your own divorce needn't be a horror if you go about it in a cool-headed, realistic, and practical way. Why is divorce usually such a mess anyhow? Because in the presence of ignorance, emotion will take over the situation every time. Get smart—get facts—and survive.

And as you will see in the pages that follow, I want a lot more for you than mere survival. You *can* come out of this stronger than ever, better organized, more self-confident, better able to shape your own destiny. There is a big, beautiful world out there waiting for you to discover it. If you do this right, you will know ever so much better how to get along well and comfortably in that world. I've seen it happen again and again. Divorce isn't fun for anyone. But if you have been just plodding along through life until now, this is the time for a total change. No more plodding for you! Reach out now, spread your wings, and learn how to fly!

Chapter 2

SURVIVAL, STAGE ONE

You ARE GOING TO SURVIVE. Planet Earth is still going round the sun. You got up this morning, and you are going to get up tomorrow morning. You are reading this book, so we know you have got some interest in what the future will bring. Before we go into the mechanics of divorce, here are some thoughts I want you to put into your head for today.

Fact: You are not going to starve to death.

Fact: You are not going to have to live in a tent. (Maybe you *want* to live in a tent, but that will be your choice.)

Fact: You are not going to find yourself suddenly without friends. You are not an outcast just because you are getting a divorce. People are really amazingly sympathetic if you give them a chance to be.

Fact: You have hidden strengths just waiting to be tested and used. Now is the time to discover them.

Fact: There are wonderful support groups all around you. If you need them, go out and find them.

Fact: Every woman worth her salt has had some crisis in her life. Dealing with gut issues is the thing that gives women their wisdom and their power. Your sisters throughout the ages have coped with situations as painful as this, and you can do it too.

Let's have a close look now at the actual process, the mechanics of divorce. Laws are in the midst of great change now throughout the United States. What in the past was usually a lawsuit for damages with great public blame attached is now being changed in state after state to a "no-fault" dissolution. Some states still demand a reason for a divorce—a specific failing or act by one party against the other—but in many areas you will find a statement on the divorce papers that simply says "During the course of my marriage there arose irrevocable differences which led to the irremediable breakdown of the marriage. There is no chance for reconciliation." And that's that.

By now you should have found out what the grounds and procedings are for divorce in your own state, and how the local family law is set up. If you are not in contact with your state commission on the status of women, try the League of Women Voters or the National Organization of Women or the American Association of University Women. They will point you in the right direction. If your area has a college or a university there is almost sure to be a department interested in this subject, and you may find a reading list or pamphlets there. In some states you can go to your county clerk and ask for the packet of forms used for divorce. There may be a small charge for these, and they may look frighteningly "legal" to you just at first, but they are worth study-ing. You will be able to discover what blanks you will be asked to fill in when you begin working with your attorney on actual filing procedures. Then you will be able to communicate far better with the person you have hired to help you sort things out.

Filing

Someone is going to file for divorce—either you or your husband. This simply means that one of you is beginning an action which will be supervised by your state in the best interests of the individuals—husband, wife, and children—and of the community involved. The person who files is called the *petitioner* and the other spouse, who must then reply either in person or through an attorney within a certain number of days, is known as the *respondent.* The court's responsibility to both husband and wife (and especially to any children involved) is to see, at this point, that both parties know of the intent to obtain a divorce and that both know what the petitioner is asking for in connection with this action. If you are the petitioner, you will probably be asking for support, child support, and equitable division of property.

Women who live in those few states that don't presently acknowledge the wife's contribution to the accumulation of family money should make a petition for fair division of it anyway! To sit back and say nothing about it at this point only pushes that day of full equality farther away.

You begin by filling out papers stating these facts and by filing these papers at the county clerk's office. Rarely will you do the actual filing—the taking of these pieces of paper to the office—yourself. This is a part of what your attorney will do for you, but you should fill out those papers yourself and know what you are doing at the time.

Maybe It Isn't Really Happening!

Let us go back to that word *filing*. If your husband says he has done this, then he has probably begun the procedure; and the date on which that first step is taken either by husband or wife has great significance. Money your husband earns from that date can be called his. It can be the date as of which we determine his, hers, ours in terms of property. This doesn't mean that you will be totally out in the cold, but it does mean that an agreement of separate maintenance must be made, usually introduced by an attorney. This document is filed with the court, and this means that things are happening. You must react within a set time, or anything proposed by your husband and not challenged by you will be accepted as final by default.

Of course you *could* stall, do nothing, and come out with a very good settlement, but this is rare. If the husband has a good deal of money and feels very guilty about leaving, it just might happen. But the economics of living usually preclude any great amount of generosity toward his present wife and family.

Do You Need an Attorney?

You need an attorney—a good one—unless you have been married two years or less and have no children and no accumulated property or accumulated debts. The do-it-yourself divorce is not for women who have been married for any length of time or who have children or property to consider.

But isn't it an extra expense, perhaps a major one? Maybe so. I still say you definitely need an attorney. You may need an injunction delivered immediately, for example, to prevent your husband from mortgaging or disposing of jointly held property. You may need to freeze a savings account until the court can decide how your cash should be divided. Depositions and/or subpoenas may be involved eventually (more on these later), and for all of these moves you will want the sort of professional advice that can save you money as well as energy and anxiety in the end.

When you file your original petition, you will be submitting a statistical form at the same time, giving information about you and your spouse: where and when you were married, who the children are and how old they are. You will state the cause for divorce ("irreconcilable difference" or other) and this information will be filed with your state bureau of statistics.

You will also be filling out a summons that will be presented personally to your husband, alerting him to your action if you are the petitioner. Usually he is required to respond to this within thirty days; otherwise the court will assume that he will not challenge any of your demands. If you are the respondent, you should proceed to make up your budget and draw up a preliminary list of your assets and liabilities (see Chapter 1) and begin as promptly as possible to search for the attorney who will do the best job of representing you.

Incidentally, there must be proof that the summons has indeed been presented, so an additional form will be prepared to be signed by the process server—the person who actually presents the summons. The court needs to know that the party concerned has been given a chance to reply. These papers are not confusing if you sit down with them quietly and have a good look at them one by one. Again, it is a matter of keeping your cool and remembering that family law was written for just such circumstances, so you are not the only one who has ever had to go through it—no matter how you may feel inside at such a moment.

The Financial Declaration

You will be asked at this time for a financial declaration as well. This form will tell all that you know about your family income and its sources plus the normal deductions from your income such as taxes and Social Security. By now you have already begun, I hope, to make up these careful lists for your Financial Notebook. In any case, don't panic: if need be, you can always file an amended declaration later on.

Some states will offer court-appointed counseling services sometimes known as mediation centers at this time. Unless you have already had extensive counseling to no avail, accept this program. It may not save the marriage, but there is a chance that it will assist you in the process of negotiating what will follow.

Your attorney is there to guide you through the maze of this paperwork, delivering the papers to the proper place at the proper time, but this is only the beginning of the job. The woman who has not been an equal partner in managing family finances (as so many have not) may find that the attorney's legal powers are necessary in order to complete the job of basic research. He or she also acts as negotiator, helping to resolve differences between your demands and claims and those of your husband. The attorney must be well able, if necessary, to represent your case in court. If agreement cannot be reached on matters of support, child custody, or settlement, you will find yourself before a judge with your point of view being put forward by the attorney you have chosen.

How to Choose Your Attorney

What do you want when you look for the right attorney to handle your divorce?

This is not the time to go running to the "old family friend" or to the lawyer who may have handled your general family or business matters in the past. This individual will be too close to the situation, and may not be informed at all about the latest laws governing divorce in your state. You want an expert now, and if it appears to you that the transaction is likely to be complicated, you may need a fighter as well. It should be someone who knows the guidelines of support and settlement in your area very thoroughly. He or she should be aware of the habits and attitudes of local judges, know courtroom techniques, and be well respected in your community.

You don't want a lawyer who has an axe to grind in favor of women—or in favor of men, either. You want your case to be handled, on its unique merits, by someone who will put *your* best interests at the top of the list. Choose an attorney who will give you a good idea of the fees that will be involved, right from the beginning. It should be someone who will respect you—not coddle you or flatter you, but treat you like a sensible and intelligent individual, getting a job done. You are going to be working with this person, perhaps for some time, on one of the most important transactions of your life. Don't make your choice on sentimental grounds, or in ignorance, or in a hurry.

How do you find such an attorney? Most areas have what is known as a lawyer's referral service, and you might begin by looking in your telephone book for this, then asking for the names of at least three attorneys who are recommended to handle divorce cases. Call their offices and ask if you might make a short appointment (say, fifteen minutes) with each of them. Sometimes there is no charge for this sort of meeting; otherwise the fee is likely to be very small. Ask direct questions during these meetings—about their experience, about fees, about time schedules. You don't want your case to be put on the back burner. You don't want anyone who seems reluctant, scornful, or disinterested.

Stay sharp and get a thorough impression of the attorney while you are doing this. Ask for references—you have a right to them. Ask around and see what you can find out about other people's impressions. Have they been satisfied with the services of this attorney? What were the circumstances? What was the outcome for the person by whom they were hired?

Don't leave it there! Call your county court and ask for the schedule for the days divorce actions will be heard. Make a point of attending court on those days and observe for yourself the style of the attorneys you see there. Are they well-prepared, well-spoken, efficient, courteous? How do they treat their clients? What seems to be the judge's reaction to their personality? To their presentation? What is the outcome for their client? A great deal can be gained from a day in court, just watching and listening. Gather impressions. You'll be grateful later on that you did.

You should be able to make a pretty good guess ahead of time as to whether or not your divorce is going to be complicated. In the average family situation with a home, cars, some stocks, bonds, and savings account, there should be no great problem about arriving at a settlement. In this case you will not need the super-sleuth trial lawyer, and you may even want to go to your local law clinic for assistance instead. The price one pays does not necessarily determine the quality of service rendered, even here. You will know in advance if there are likely to be added complications—if you are going to be dealing with a mixture of separate and community properties, for example—or if you will need to determine something difficult like the value of good will in a small, family-owned company. In any case, get the best estimate you can on the cost to be expected when you have made your final choice of the attorney who is going to represent you. Then be prepared to watch the time spent, the number of letters going back and forth, the documents produced, and keep track of anything extra such as court appearances and depositions that may come along. You will have a basis for discussing any questions later about the attorney's fees if you have been watchful from the beginning. And ask for a monthly statement. Look it over regularly and see if it tallies with your own estimates.

Here is an example of what I am talking about. Gertrude was in shock when she saw her attorney's final bill for $15,000. She remembered that $75 an hour was the agreed-upon fee, and they had not had to go to court (which would have been extra). She concluded that the bill represented two hundred hours: five weeks of work on nothing but her case at forty hours per week. She had no figures to show why she doubted such a thing had actually taken place. What could she do? Not much. The local bar association interests itself in abuses, of course, but they had better be well-documented.

On the negative side, there are some attorneys who are less than careful about ordering expensive procedures such as depositions that may not be really necessary. (A deposition is a formal questioning, under oath, of a party in a legal situation but not in court. It costs extra for attorneys' time, for a professional stenographer, and for transcription.) Sometimes this may turn up important evidence, particularly when funds have been concealed from the wife who was not a partner in family money management. In other instances, we may well question the motive. It may be the client who has brought it on herself by coming to her attorney in a highly emotional state, saying that she wants to fight over every penny no matter what the cost. This doesn't make much sense. You *can* try to create an atmosphere in which you and your husband may be able to come to an agreement about support and settlement of family assets. He may not go along, but it will do you no harm to be as gracious as you can. In working with your lawyer, remember that the actual decisions at every step are up to you.

How Much Should It Cost?

There is no easy answer to this question. At the end of the first interview, the attorney usually presents a fee schedule to the client, listing per-hour fees such as perhaps $50 for office visits, $50 an hour for phone calls, $45 for reviewing, and so forth. But the problem is to try and get some idea of how long all this is going to take. We know that there will be time for consulting the husband's attorney, time for court appearances, papers to be filed; but the attorney should be asked to give an estimate of what it may cost altogether *if no unexpected problems arise*.

A frank discussion should be held about any "extra services" that may be billed, and at all times you should be on top of the question as to whether or not these services are really necessary. You have a right to have each point explained to you, just as you would if you were hiring a gardener or a plumber to do something that you cannot do. Be sure of your own motives when you go along with the idea of extra services. If you are paying for a search into the possibility of hidden moneys, don't do it just for spite. Spite doesn't pay. Don't do it if you can sit down with a paper and pencil and figure out that the hidden money is probably less than the cost to you of finding it! I have seen a good many women indulge in wishful thinking about nonexistent secret money in divorce situations. Try to make up your mind early: do you believe, realistically, that investments have been made without your knowledge? Have businesses been sold without a trace of what happened to the funds? Could money have been placed in a bank under another person's name? Only you can decide whether this is likely to be true and whether or not you want to go for it.

Tax Laws and Attorneys

Watch out for a tricky business of padding expenses in connection with the desire of the divorcing husband and wife to escape taxes. Spousal support (alimony) is tax-deductible for the person paying that money. Husbands in the higher income brackets sometimes send the wife's attorney's fees to the wife, changing fees to support money in name only, and advising the wife to forward them to the attorney. In return, the attorney lists his fees mostly as having to do with tax and investment advice, which in turn is deductible for the wife. It sounds beautiful, but it isn't. Too often the fees themselves in these cases begin ballooning. No person involved should have to pay excessive costs, whatever the tax consequences.

You Make Your Lawyer Great

You make your lawyer great by being an efficient, well-informed client who consistently supplies the hard facts necessary for him or her to conduct the case. Once you have chosen a good attorney, a great deal of what happens next is up to you.

It is very hard for many women to *hear* at this point what is being said to them. Emotion gets in the way. Thoughts are in a turmoil. Reality flies out the window, and time and energy and money are being wasted. You make your lawyer great by being a good listener. Every time you talk with this professional adviser of yours, write things down. Go in with a list and come out with another list. Keep these papers filed in your Financial Notebook under *Divorce.* Date them. Check off the items that have been taken care of, then go after the ones you still have to do.

Remember, in dealing with your lawyer, that no one in a divorce is going to get every wish satisfied. As long as you are certain that your counsel is working for you, there is no use howling because your husband always said "Maude, I will take care of you forever." There is no sense crying over all you did for him, year after year. Instead, ask "What does the law say?" and ask "How is that law usually interpreted?" Ask "What is your past experience of the court's response to this sort of situation?" and ask "What possibilities do we have of bargaining in this place where we certainly don't agree?" If you force yourself to do this, you will learn a great deal very fast, and you will find that you are working in a much more comfortable partnership with your attorney.

Presenting the Facts

You have made up a good many lists by now, and you have filled out the basic forms for the filing of divorce. You have figured out what it has been costing you to live, and you have submitted these figures to the court. Now you can help your attorney to take the next steps by sitting down to write out a brief history of the financial events in your marriage as well as you can remember them. Into this narrative you can also put relevant information about attitudes and experiences with direct bearing on the *financial transaction of divorce:* but keep it factual and stay cool. You are not writing *Gone with the Wind,* just a neatly collected series of events, well enough expressed so that your attorney will find them useful.

Record things chronologically. When did you marry? Were you working at the time? If so, what did you earn? What was your educational background, your level of achievement? Did you continue to work after marriage? What property, jewelry, personal possessions of value did you have at the time of the marriage? Did you help support your husband while he finished school, while he was between jobs? How much did he make when you married him? Later? Did he change jobs—if so, when? How did you bank your money—together or separately? Did you save for some special purpose? How about children? Were you supporting anyone's parents or other relatives? Do you expect any inheritance in the next five years? Have you received any gifts or inheritance that might be a point of contention?

It will help to record, too, what the attitudes about money have been. Were you spenders or savers? Was he a man who expected you to get along on a minuscule household budget while he played the real estate market? Did either or both of you tend to get into debt? All of this will be very helpful to your attorney in any dealings with the other side, in or out of court. It may well provide the basis for a better level of support and/or a better settlement, if such facts are known.

This is a time when events of the past are whirling around in your head in a state of confusion. All the more reason for putting things down on paper where you can have a good look at them. Chances are you will find something in that narrative to be proud of. You will definitely see things you hadn't really considered before. Now you are looking at the whole picture with a new sense of control and therefore a better level of self-esteem. You are giving yourself a little free therapy here, and at the same time you are helping your attorney to do the best possible job for you.

You understand by now why I want you to *write things down!* It's the best habit you can possibly develop at this point, from the practical and the psychological point of view. You have another job ahead of you right now, but first look at all the written material you have in front of you by now and congratulate yourself. Do something nice for yourself today, while you're at it. We're about to turn the big corner from The Past to The Future. Take a walk or a soak in the tub. Have lunch with a friend. Fix your hair a new way. Think

\ings you really like about yourself (and write
\vn!). Think of six things you've done to make
\ue world a little better place for others, and write them
down too. Nobody has to see these lists, but you will
know what's in them, and that will help.

Planning for Your Future

It's too soon for most of you to come up with
the definitive Twenty-Year Plan right now, but it's a
good time to begin working on it. The next stage of
your divorce proceedings is going to require a detailed
budget from you, showing the rock-bottom cost of supporting yourself and your children. The papers you filed
showed what you used to spend. You hope, of course,
that this standard of living can be maintained. But you
must face the fact now that it is only the very rare
situation where this can be true.

A divorce almost always means a drop in the standard of living for both parties. How are you going to
manage? Before you go any farther, you should know
your minimum requirements and be able to keep them
firmly in mind during negotiations.

If you have done a good job on the Financial Notebook we worked on in the preceding chapter, this is
where you can really put it to work for you. Go over
your monthly expenses carefully and label all those
items of expense that clearly cannot be changed. For
example, there is the cost of shelter. Presumably you
are still in the family home and no decisions have yet
been made about a move. How much does it cost you
to live in your house? Look at mortgage, utilities, insurance costs, and don't forget upkeep and maintenance.
Now, what is the cost of food? Of basic transportation?
Many of these items would be hard to change.

But there may be items that you took for granted
that are really nonessentials. Can you cut down on

clothes, on entertainment, on gifts? Look at everything that is not an absolute necessity, and think it over. This is where we will trim and shape your budget for the days to come.

Try to avoid emotionalizing about this, by all means. It isn't pleasant, but it is good for you because you are facing reality and making choices before they are forced on you. Remember, you won't have to do without forever. In time you will find ways of raising money to get these things back into your life, if you really want them. This is a temporary austerity program that will give you knowledge, and in knowledge there is security.

In most cases, the husband is required by the court to pay at least temporary support for his ex-wife and family. True, this is his moral obligation, but remember that there are limits to the demands you can place upon him. Judges take into account the fact that the wage-earner must be allowed to keep a good percentage of what he makes in order to have any incentive to work at all. Totally unreasonable demands on your part will only work against your best interests in the long run. Too many men simply walk away from a divorce and can't be found, if the terms are too harsh. The number of women living without any support at all from former spouses is quite appalling. You must think calmly and creatively about a system that is going to work for you.

While you're at it, consider the fact that your husband could be in much worse shape than you are right now, emotionally. (It's a real possibility!) Men have a hard time talking to other men, as a general rule. Many don't read books and magazines telling them what is happening outside of the walled castles they call "work." They talk to colleagues within that walled city where no one is apt to know about the changes in divorce laws, alimony laws, division of property. The man throws himself at his friend The Lawyer, whose spe-

ciality may not even be in family law, but no matter—
this is his good old buddy and he assumes the man
will get him through a perfectly smooth operation. He
imagines that he will offer his ex-wife something or
other, and that will be that.

Then comes the day of reckoning. The judge says
"George, you must pay temporary alimony since this
woman has no way of supporting herself"—he hadn't
thought of that. He says "George, now we are going to
divide up the property." *Divide up the property? Didn't
I earn it all?* George is in shock. Some of the things
that are going to happen in the next few months will
be a direct result of this shock and the emotional state
the man is now in. It may take as long as a year, or
more, for George's attorney to convince him that his
wife is going to receive half of all the assets ("But I
made all the money—she was just a housewife—she
never *worked*") and that she is going to receive adequate support for herself and their children while she
prepares herself to enter the job market again, or perhaps for the very first time.

Why Temporary Support?

Some areas have developed guidelines for attorneys and judges to use in determining the amount of
support (child support, spousal support—the latter also
known as alimony) appropriate in a given situation.
These guidelines are not absolutes, but are suggestions
based on the amount of income available. It usually
begins with the salary of the wage-earning husband,
with acknowledgments of any income from paid work
of the wife. It also takes into consideration the ages
of the children and the work experience, if any, of the
wife. Rarely and only in extraordinary circumstances
would 50 percent of income be allotted to the wife and
children. Alimony, or spousal support, in more and
more states is now awarded on a temporary basis in

order to provide a time of adjustment for the woman who must now go outside the home to work.

If you have been a housewife all your life, this may seem harsh to you, and you may not like what I am going to tell you. *I want women to work!* And I mean even the rare woman who will still have enough income after divorce, so that she could sit back instead and watch the world go by. The wealthiest women I have advised have had to hear me say this, and when they work with me on their finances, I give them plenty of tough assignments right from the start. It doesn't have to be a paid job if they are lucky enough to have that choice. I do want it to be something useful, something that will give that woman a real sense of participation in events, of achievement she can be proud of. A lazy woman is an unsatisfied person and she is boring to all about her. She has no chance to grow. I don't want to spend my time with her, and neither do you.

So don't waste time feeling sorry for yourself if you have to enter the job market for financial reasons. Use that energy instead to do some creative brainstorming about the sort of work you'd like to do, and how you can find a way of getting paid for it. Recent studies show that you'll make more money if you do a job that really appeals to you. Look at this as an opportunity to develop skills you never knew you had, to meet people you never would have known in your other life, and to find new ways of becoming the bigger and better person you were meant to be. We'll come back to the subject of re-entry in depth in a later chapter, but this is the time to begin developing your ideas on the subject, for more than one reason.

First of all, it's good for you. Second, if your attorney and your husband's attorney cannot come to a simple agreement about the terms of your separation and support, then you will have to appear briefly in court. When you go to court on this round, you will do a great deal better if you are ready to speak up with the bare outlines, at least, of a plan for your future. Your plan can be changed later, of course. But it will be greatly to your advantage if you can say "I am investigating the possibility of going into real estate sales" or "I am setting up interviews with business acquaintances" or "I'm going back to school to study such-and-such job skills." You mustn't sit there and sniffle and look helpless at a moment like this. It's much better to show that you are an individual taking charge of her own life, a person in her own right, worthy of respect.

If You Go to Court

This preliminary visit to court is not going to paralyze you if you prepare yourself for it. Make a list of your questions and have a brief, well-organized session with your attorney about exactly what to expect. If you have not already been there looking over attorneys, go to the courthouse a day or two ahead of time. Find out where to park your car. Find out how to get to the floor or department you are going to be looking for. Find out where the women's room is and where to get a drink of water or a cup of coffee and a snack.

Don't go to court alone. Ask a good, calm, reliable friend to drive you there well ahead of time on the day you are to appear. Have him or her sit in the court and observe, to give you feedback later. Your attorney will have advised you about the procedures and about any specific questions that may arise. Tell the truth, be brief, be dignified. Whatever your emotions may be, save them for later. When your friend drives you home afterward, you can cry or laugh all you want.

What Next?

You are now legally separated, and if all has gone reasonably well, you have a temporary system of support in working order. Now that you are to receive a stated amount for spousal support it is your responsibility to file IRS Form 1040-ES, obtained from your local Internal Revenue Service Office. This form will show you how to estimate your income tax based on your expected spousal support and any other income. You will be instructed to pay that tax quarterly, January 15, April 15, July 15 and October 15. You have the beginnings of a Financial Notebook; you are preparing your thoughts about the new way of life ahead of you. What next?

For many women there is an emotional let-down at this point. Don't be too surprised if it happens to you. A lot of energy has been put into understanding what is happening. Adrenaline was high while you were organizing yourself to meet these challenges. The attorney helped you to feel that somehow everything was going to be all right. Now that the first shock of it all is over, you wonder again—*why?* Could I have done anything differently? What were my faults? How did I fail? Loneliness closes in. The unknown future is demoralizing. That old sense of helplessness and panic very often strikes again.

What to do? You will need some sort of support group, although this need not be a formal situation if you can find it in other ways. Your family, your close friends, your church can help. Be honest about asking for what you need. If this includes a psychiatric therapist for a time or a course of group therapy sessions, fine. Do what is necessary *now*—don't put it off. There is usually a lull in the action while both sides in the divorce prepare for negotiation of property settlement. So much the better. This gives you a chance to tend to your personal needs. Grieving and complaining now may be a very practical move on your part toward future growth. Just be sure you are getting it over with, doing a thorough job of it, and not going over and over the same material endlessly.

If you go for professional help, here is a warning. Unless you are clinically ill, look on this as something very temporary. The weekly or twice-weekly appointment with a sympathetic listener is helpful and it spares your friends if you are beginning to become a hopeless bore. But don't let it prevent you from learning as soon as possible to stand on your own feet. Just as there are a few unscrupulous attorneys (and irresponsible people in every other group), there are people in the healing professions who will be interested in continuing your appointments indefinitely. If you have been dependent on your husband for emotional support, beware of transferring this dependency to another person, professional or not. You don't want to find yourself in an emotional bind all over again. When you hire a doctor, you are the boss in this situation too. You are not there to see that his mortgage gets paid. You are there to get yourself healed and the professional may be able to give you some tips, but only you can do the job in the long run.

Use this help with caution. Refuse the offer of prescriptions for tranquilizers. Experts in loss and bereavement tell us that these only delay the natural process, and help to bury grief in a place where it will come back to haunt you later. I hope you know by now that liquor is to be avoided during any time of crisis. You may think it helps to make you feel better, but it really depresses you. It is dangerous stuff. I know I am lecturing and moralizing, but I want you to understand that you must not get hooked on *anything* at this point— and that includes drugs, booze, and psychiatry. If only from a practical point of view, you have to realize that it's a dangerous business to be paying out money, running up debts, for anything you can do without, if doing without means standing on your own two feet.

Better to invest, if you want to spend money on yourself right now, in a gym course or a good, vigorous exercise class. If your budget doesn't permit that, go out walking, jogging, running—which is free and great for your health.

How about dates? It's a no-fault divorce, after all, and it would be nice to have another man telling you that you are still attractive and desirable. You'd like to show your husband a thing or two—wouldn't you? Don't be dumb. Protect yourself. You are in a very vulnerable position at the moment, and you don't need more trouble than you already have going for you. Hold off for a good many months on this kind of socializing, and check on the rules very carefully with your attorney. Even in some of the no-fault states, evidence of adultery on the part of the wife may seriously affect the outcome of the settlement. Your most innocent actions may be misconstrued, right now. Don't take chances. You'll be doing yourself a big favor, from an emotional point of view, if you make up your mind to go your own way independently, suffer the loneliness, and get it over with *before* you enter into any intimate relationship with another man.

This *is* going to be over someday, and when it is over you are going to know a great deal more about who you are. You are going to know that you can make it on your own. *Men are great, but so are you!* Your next relationship is going to be based not on need but on equal sharing and equal commitment by two independent human beings.

You don't believe me? Well, wait and see. Someday you are going to be looking for a man seven feet tall, because that's how powerful and capable you yourself are going to feel.

Chapter 3

THE INTERIM

Y OU ARE NOW at the stage in the divorce process that I think of as The Interim. You have filled out and filed the preliminary papers, you have chosen your attorney, you have begun a careful investigation of your financial situation, and you have arranged for temporary support. What next?

I can't give you a reliable time schedule for the series of events that are going to follow, because there isn't one. Each divorce is different. A great deal depends on the nature of the assets to be divided in the settlement and how complicated that procedure is likely to be. A great deal depends on the attitudes of the husband and wife involved. Whatever the problems, however, begin now with some comprehensive plans for your own future. We are going to take it here, step by step. Some women will be so frightened by the fact of divorce that they blind themselves to the necessity of making a plan. They put it off and put it off, thinking that if they really have a look at the facts they will find something terrible. They feel so negative about the future that they don't want to deal with it in any form.

Don't let yourself get stuck in this set of attitudes! So, you can't live at the same economic level you have been used to. You may be in for a surprise: the next level down may prove much happier. Once you get your act together, you may find that it even offers you more security. Poor is a state of mind. You don't have to be in it. Force yourself, if necessary at first, to take charge of your future with pencil and paper in hand. You can always change your plan around later on, if you need to. The important thing is to get started, to be active, to be in motion.

Cash

If you are getting a support check you won't want to hold your breath each month waiting for it to come and wasting energy on being terrified. You will need a backup fund for emergencies. If you have a joint savings account, I suggest that you take one half of that account and place that amount in your name in another bank, so that the two accounts won't be confused. You are not stealing anything. You are merely moving what is already yours to a place where you know that you (and only you) can get at it. This withdrawal will show on the record and you will be sure to state it on your list of assets when the time comes for negotiation, but in the meantime it will give you peace of mind. There is nothing more demoralizing than being totally without funds at a time like this if something happens to the car or the hot water heater blows. Warning: This is *emergency money*. It is a cushion to rely on. Don't spend a cent of it for frivolous purposes! If the support check is late and you have turned to this fund to pay ordinary living expenses, the amount should be replaced immediately.

If you have a savings account which is in your husband's name alone, ask your attorney *now* to arrange a division of that account. We don't want Joe to go up and buy a new car for himself with funds that by rights belong to both of you. A possible exception to this rule might arise if your husband needs this cash available to keep his business going. If so, move gently and be reasonable. Nothing should jeopardize his continued ability to earn a living. Remember that his financial future is also yours as long as you and/or your children continue to receive support from him. You, in turn, should be as supportive as possible of his business interests.

If at this time you feel that cash or other assets might be misused (spent for things other than family necessities), consult your lawyer. If need be, a court order known as an *injunction* can be placed on these moneys and properties so that nothing whatever can be done with them in the absence of a further court order giving permission. Freezing your assets may in some circumstances be the only way to preserve them for future use.

If the Support Check Is Late

If the support check is more than a few days late, you should be in touch with your attorney about it immediately. I do not advise complaining to your husband about this sort of thing directly. This only brings emotion back into the picture, in the delicate area of money management. People sometimes forget what they want to forget, and in this case they need to be reminded—but not by you.

Maintaining Your Credit

One of your new responsibilities will be to maintain your credit during the present time of transition. I am saying *maintain* your credit rather than *establish* it, for if you have had a good credit rating during the time when you were married, you can use that rating to continue credit in your own name. You will have to fill out forms of application, stating the truth about your finances. Remind the companies to check your rating under your married name. If you are turned down, ask to see the reasons in writing. The law now states that you should have credit if your estimated income and job situation warrant it. Whether or not you ever earned a dime during your marriage, you were a full partner in that enterprise and you deserve the benefits of it.

Paula had only worked at her new job for three months, and when she applied for credit she was refused. Then an interesting thing happened. She decided to send in another application, but this time she forgot to add the "a" at the end of her name. As "Paul" rather than "Paula" with all the other information being equal, she received credit this time around. Did she sue? No. But if a great many other women hadn't gone out and fought this battle, we wouldn't have the fair credit-rating practices that we have today. The law states equality in this area, but it is taking time for it to filter down to the individual clerk who may be handling your application. Speak up and demand your rights if they are denied.

Facing Facts about Your Support Money

The women I work with in divorce situations may be receiving anything from a few hundred to several thousand dollars a month in support, but the principle on which I advise them is always the same. No matter how lavish or how meager it may be, I want them to understand that this support is temporary and that the situation in which they find themselves right now is bound to change. In terms of your own support money, the time to look ahead is now, not later. Again, work with paper and pencil in hand.

Let's look at Jeanette's situation. She is forty-two and has three teen-aged children. On the basis of a plan to re-educate herself and to re-enter the job market in a period of three to four years, she has won a judgment of $800-a-month support for the next four years for herself and $150 per month until they are eighteen for each of the children. Her husband makes about $35,000 a year and there is some property involved which has not yet been divided. Jeanette makes a chart for herself, so that she can see clearly what to expect and what *not* to expect as the years go by:

Jeanette's Support Chart

	1981	82	83	84	85	86	87	88	89	90
Jeanette 42	800	800	800	800/						
Jim 15	150	150	150/							
Susie 12	150	150	150	150	150	150/				
Ted 10	150	150	150	150	150	150	150	150/		
Total	1250	1250	1250	1100	300	300	150	150	0	

Jeanette now understands that there will be a major change in the amount of support when each child reaches eighteen, and she sees that the crucial year will be 1986, when only $300 a month will be coming in to support her and the two remaining children. She also knows that very few children are able to support themselves at the age of eighteen, so she must be able to take up the burden by means of her own earnings by that time. A chart such as this will tell Jeanette something about her housing plans as well. The year 1985 may be the time when she will plan to move from the present home to an efficient apartment.

Let's be realistic. Those grand plans of so many years ago, Jim going on to Harvard and Susie studying music at Juilliard, may have to be modified now. Perhaps there will be scholarships available. Your children will not lack education if their talent warrants it, but the funding of it all may very well have to be done in an unanticipated manner.

"But, their father will continue to help them after they are eighteen! He would do anything for them—he loves them dearly!" I hear this sort of thing so often. Don't be too sure of it. In fact, don't be sure of it at all. If he marries again (and statistics tell us that he is very likely to) there will be other influences working on him. Soon he may have another family to support. Great pressure may be upon him to finish his obligation to your children as soon as the law allows.

"But he is going to be worth more money later on—it isn't fair!" I agree; it isn't fair. I have always thought that children should enjoy benefits when their father increases his income or receives an inheritance and thus increases his ability to pay. When you are negotiating child support, you would be well advised to try for a percentage of his income rather than a flat sum and to take into account the possibility of future renegotiating in view of inflation, too. Especially if the children are capable and highly motivated, you will want to protect their educational prospects as well as possible. The use of trusts can be suggested. You may even wish to offer a cut in present support if, in exchange, certain amounts are put into a safely invested fund to be used later for educational purposes.

Remember, though, while you are putting together your thoughts on this subject that the wage-earner must be allowed to keep enough money for decent living on his own, or the incentive dies. If too much of his money is allotted to former spouse and children, he just may decide to retire or to leave town. Judges will also look at the sums of money or property being transferred to the wife. If these are large, support is likely to be smaller. If this happens, you may have to invade your capital on a regular basis for ordinary living expenses, and there goes your old-age security. My point is not that you can't win but that the whole process involves compromise. We will go into the business of negotiation in a later chapter, but understand now that it is to your own advantage to keep a cool head, a gracious demeanor, and a clear view of the long-term situation from the beginning.

Before we go on to talk about your living arrangements and your future job, a few more words about the issue of support. I have had women come to me and say "But I am blameless and he can well afford it: I am going to have *lifetime support.*" I tell them that there is no such thing.

Think about it. Any individual who is being supported by the labor of another person must realize that the support comes in only as long as that other person has the funds or the ability to earn them. The individual who is dependent in this way has very little to say about her own future, when you come right down to it. Let me give you an outstanding example. A middle-aged woman came to me recently for advice looking as if she was going to come apart at the seams any minute. "This one is in *real* trouble," I thought.

"My husband wants a divorce!" Mrs. A. told me, in tears. Well, I had heard that many times—but then she told me that they had been separated for fourteen years! This was a shocker. I couldn't recall ever having seen a longer separation. I will probably never know the reasons that kept this couple from reconstituting their marriage or else going through with the final actions necessary for divorce. Evidently he did not have any wish to remarry, and neither did she. There was a gleam in her eye when she told me how much support money he had been paying her all these years—well, maybe she had "shown him." But what did she really show him? Now she was in her fifties, and her husband was ready to retire. No longer would there be a large income for him to share with her. Due to the generosity of this man and of the court she had been led into a trap.

Mrs. A. had no children. She should have been *released* from being a dependent, long ago. It would have been far better for her in the long run if she had been given only enough support to give her an opportunity to retrain and become self-sufficient. She should have begun a new life at the age of thirty-six, when she originally parted from the man. Her chances would have been very much better then.

The anguish of divorce for the middle-aged woman is that she must begin all over again, competing with younger, stronger, and better-trained individuals in a world that has been foreign to her all these years. She sees her husband walk away from the marriage taking with him his long-proved ability to earn a living, his business reputation, his professional expertise. Very likely he will continue to increase his earning power. She meantime will be given an amount of support rapidly eaten away by inflation, with no very likely prospect of suing for more. Lawsuits to increase support generally add only to the incomes of the attorneys involved. For the older woman who has been a dependent all her life, this is a heartbreaking situation.

Younger women, be warned—and older women, take heart. We all know of the females in this world who have "done the impossible." They rolled up their sleeves and got the job done, no matter what it was. They created shops and services, they farmed, they ran boardinghouses, they used their experience of running a family to enter the larger world at an executive level—they did what they had to do, to survive. The women of the 1980s can do the same thing if they know what the score is, and if they see the challenges ahead of them as opportunities.

The main thing is not to sit back and accept that support check in a passive frame of mind. Create some goals for yourself instead—short-term goals and long-term goals, all of them flexible as they need to be; but have faith in yourself. Make up your mind to be a part of humanity, to take pride in your work, whatever it is, to be stimulated by new experiences. This is what creates the fascinating woman! You may not want to believe it just at this moment, but if you do what I suggest, you will soon be far more interesting as a person than you have ever been. You may even find that your husband wants you back, in time—and then you take another look at him and decide that he is a terrible bore.

Where Am I Going to Live?

We are still talking about The Interim, and I advise you not to make any sudden moves just at this moment. But, looking at the support schedule in front of you, especially if you have children, you should begin to plan very carefully now for the long-term future. Where are they in school? This may be the determining factor for you at present. Perhaps it would be best to stay near that school where Jimmy is getting along so well and where he is receiving such a superior education. Just keep in mind that it won't be forever. And keep in mind your own development. Is the right school for *you* near enough by? What are the possibilities of training or employment in your neighborhood? You owe your children a great deal, but the number-one thing you owe them is a happy parent. Think of your own future while you are thinking of theirs. Give yourself a little time to get on your feet emotionally, but if you feel it would be better in terms of opportunity for you to move in six months or a year, then start planning that move.

In Chapter 5 we take a careful look at real estate management, after which you will have a better basis for deciding whether or not you ought to stay in the family home. Right here, though, we must recognize the fact that "home" is a very powerful item in a woman's life. The psychological effects of it, and of the security it offers, must not be ignored. The house and its furnishing are more than material objects to the average female. They are an extension of her own body, which has offered shelter to the man in her life and to the children she has borne. The home is her nest and her refuge; leaving it, she is likely to feel terribly exposed and amputated. During the worst of the emotional crisis of divorce, it may be worth spending money "unwisely" just to keep her in it for a time at least. Indeed, she may decide that many other benefits can be sacrificed to this need for remaining in the place that is safe and known—and her sacrifice may turn out to be wise after all, in terms of the strength she derives from it. It makes sense to go ahead and live in the place that works best for you, as long as that place is available. Just don't do it unconsciously! Know what is involved, what you are really reacting to. Then you can make your own choices and be prepared to take the consequences.

What about My Community?

This is a good time to ask yourself "What *is* my community?" Does it consist of family, of friends, of members of a church or a club group? What do my neighbors mean to me? It is time to look at the economic standards of those around you and ask yourself whether or not you want to put a great deal of energy into trying to live up to that. Don't make financial decisions based on anyone's standards but your own. Your true friends will be those who care for the person you are. In front of your family and whatever group you call your true *community,* you shouldn't have to keep up appearances.

If the circumstances of your marriage have left you in a "keep-up-with-the-Joneses" financial trap, you might consider moving to another neighborhood for a fresh start. Again, however, don't do anything hastily. Just keep this in mind as a possibility and realize that you are free now to do it, if that is really what you want to do. Whenever we think of the disadvantages of divorce, which are very real and often very painful, we have to think of the advantages as well. You don't have to live somewhere now because your husband's company has stationed him there, or because this is the place he chose.

His Plan for Her

When couples have been married for some years, very often the husband is accustomed to making plans for the entire family. Divorce comes, and this man conscientiously believes that he will go right on doing the same thing. In one case I know of, "Father" told "Mother" not to worry: he had filed for divorce but she would "always be taken care of." From his point of view, that is exactly what he meant. He had met with his lawyer, who had set the wheels in motion for him, and now he sat down to plan the rest of his wife's life for her.

She had never been a demanding woman. She had been a splendid manager, eking out a very good standard of living on the small household allowance he had handed over to her. Fortunately, she had developed no expensive tastes. So, he thought, with a nominal sum given to her each month she could continue to live quite well, couldn't she? He would take some of the money they had saved and buy a small house he had seen on his last visit to the children's neighborhood. She would like to live near them! They would look after her and that would ease his anxiety. It really was an adequate house, and the money he *gave* her each month would serve to *take care of her.*

The woman in question was appalled. Despite the nature of this marriage, she had a strong enough self-image. She went out and researched the divorce laws in her state to find out what was due her for her years *in partnership* with this man to whom she had been united in holy matrimony. "Mother" soon found out that she could be supported during the time it would take her to re-educate herself so that she could become the new person she intended to be. This would take time, but she made a plan. She would go back to school, taking one year for refresher courses, and meantime she would consult a professional career counselor to help her develop an appropriate position for herself in the wage-earning world.

"Mother" was going to move, yes—but she was going to take a smart little apartment near the local college campus, not a dingy cottage near the kids. She was going to look after herself, thank you—and the children could do the same. By now she realized that she was entitled to one half of the assets she and her husband had acquired during their twenty years of marriage. She had taken time to make a careful list of everything they owned. She had hired an accountant to explain each of these assets to her, and she had decided which ones would be of benefit to her in her new life-style. She was not going to be *given* anything whatever in a condescending manner. She was going to *take* what already belonged to her, and walk away.

Her husband's lawyer did not, evidently, tell him

that the bone he was throwing to "Mother" was likely to prove unacceptable in terms of the newer laws regarding divorce. When she presented her proposal, "Father" was in a worse state of shock than she had ever been. It would take time for him to understand that her plans were not only lawful but entirely sensible. Hadn't *he* earned all that money? After all, *she had never worked.* Sorry, Dad, the courts in most states now don't see it that way.

Her Plan for Herself

Now, what about you? First, let your imagination fly! List some of those things you dreamed of doing long ago. List things you are good at doing, and put stars next to the ones you most enjoy. Reach high with your ambitions just at first—there will be time enough for you to come down to reality. Don't underestimate yourself at this point. This interim is the time to explore your fantasy future with yourself, with your best friends and advisers, with a support group and/or a trained counselor if necessary. Give yourself a number of weeks, or several months, if possible, to learn about your potential. Then begin settling into a practical plan.

If schooling is needed, find out about the courses and the time involved. Make a budget to show the cost, including the price of transportation, child care, and the like, if needed. List books, tuition, incidental expenses. Look into the possibility of financial aid through the school or college, with the help of their staff.

If a training course in a business or profession is your choice, get the details of this down on paper too. You are going to have to sell your former husband (and perhaps the court) on this entire program—it won't be handed to you on a silver platter. The more facts you have at your fingertips, the better your chances are going to be. *Is it a silly idea? After all, I've been a house-*

wife all these years! Well, you had better believe that it is not a silly idea at all. People of all ages are going back to college now. If you want to learn how to be a veterinarian or an insurance broker, go out and do it. You might even want to learn how to fly an airplane. Why not? Keep in mind, even if you are now past forty, that the average woman of our times will be *active* when she is eighty years old. *What do you want to be doing then?* If it takes you five years either to obtain that degree you need for an adequate salary or to start a small business, knowing that minimum income can be expected for some time, you should reach out for the chance.

Remember, your plan is not carved in granite. It can be changed, if your needs or opportunities change. The important thing is to develop a plan so that you are acting and not reacting when it comes time for the final settlement of this divorce. It should be *your* plan, not "Father's" plan. The financial settlement is not going to do you any good unless it buys you what you really need and want. The secret of financial management is not to work for money, but to make your money work for you.

How to Handle Yourself during The Interim

Every divorce situation will be different, of course. Yet I see enough patterns recurring over and over again to make me want to give you a few tips on what is likely to happen during this period after the first round and before the final settlement. If you go wrong at this point, you are likely to set yourself up for unnecessary later losses, both financial and emotional. Some of this has to do with manners and some of it with people-management. It's hard to do either well at a time when you are quite naturally upset. If you know what to expect, maybe it will help you to keep your cool.

What I see happening very often is a scenario something like this:

AT SIX WEEKS: "Why, we are getting along so well! It wasn't as bad as I expected when he actually moved out, and he has already sent me a check. He is seeing the children every weekend, and being so nice to them!"

SIX MONTHS LATER: "That dirty dog! My check is late! He takes the kids and gives them anything they want. He lets them eat junk food; he gives them stupid, inappropriate presents. He has money to show them a good time and I can hardly make it on what he gives us. I have to do all the discipline, but he is trying to buy their love. Not only that, he has taken all my favorite books and records. He even wants the slides we took on our last holiday! I'll get him! I'll change the locks. . . ." And so on.

SIX MONTHS LATER THAN THAT: Where do I get the money for a new roof at this point? He says that I can have the house and go out to work, and that's that. The kids are impossible and I need a vacation. I haven't held down a job outside the home for fifteen years. His lawyer calls up my lawyer and yells. Now he says he doesn't owe me a thing. He said he'd always take care of me and now I know the bastard never loved me to begin with. He couldn't have, if he's treating me this way now. I can't stand it. . . ."

Well, wouldn't it be wonderful if we could have continued being reasonable. Unfortunately, life very often isn't, and neither are we. It is easy merely to write a check. It is not so easy to give up years of living together, and to divide up property is to divide up hopes and memories as well. You will do better if you know ahead of time that others have gone through this painful kind of emotional infighting. Be prepared, and do the very best you can to curb your tongue. Don't seek revenge, either in words or in actions. Hold your course, keep smiling, and count on time to be the healer. You are going to seek the best settlement you can get, knowing that you are not *taking,* you are demanding *your share.* You are going to stand up tall and proud, and to do this you needn't be aggressive. You just need to be firm with yourself and others around you, without unpleasantness of any kind.

When you have any conversations with your husband, keep them simple. Learn to answer briefly when a question is asked. Learn to say "yes," "no," "thank you," and "that is interesting." Don't *chat.* Don't *explain.* Especially when you are talking about money, don't get long-winded. The minute too many things are discussed at once, the water gets muddy. The minute you say "because" you are inviting an argument. Why should you give a reason? If you are really going to be on your own now, you don't have to go into all that. If he asks you a question to which you don't know the answer, simply say "I don't know"—period. Most of your final negotiation is going to be in the hands of the attorneys, true. But you can do a great deal now to establish an atmosphere in which to negotiate fairly and sensibly.

And you must not try to crawl inside anyone else's head at this point, especially not your former husband's. Some women become almost paranoid during this time of strain. In discussions with their lawyers they say "But I know exactly what he is going to say about that proposal . . . about custody . . . about spousal support." They don't know at all! By now, he too is receiving a great deal of pressure from other sources, a great deal of advice, information, and misinformation. Don't jump the gun. Stop what is really only guessing, and wait instead for the logic of events to unfold.

Here are some other don'ts for The Interim period:

1. Don't expect anyone else, not *anyone,* to understand entirely what you are feeling. No matter how many divorces there have been in the world before, this one is just a little bit different.

2. Don't drop any of your major decisions on your family, and don't borrow money from your parents at this point. They may want to be very supportive, but accept their love or an outright gift, and nothing else. Too often parents lend money to the children in times of need without really being able to afford it. Only accept help if you know that it never needs to be repaid.

3. Don't lean on your children. "I could never do that," you say. Oh, yes, you could. When a woman feels desperately lonely and terribly hurt, even small children are used in this fashion. Are you using your children to pass messages to your husband? To express your own feelings and attitudes? Stop it! If you must communicate with him, do it yourself. Or do it through your attorney, not through the kids. If they come home with a loaded message such as "Dad couldn't take us out to dinner because he's so poor now—he doesn't have any money," just say "That's interesting" and let the subject drop. Children are not stupid, and they will soon learn not to bring these messages any more if they see that you are not going to be concerned.

Children and Finances

I firmly believe that family finances have to be managed by adults. If, in the divorce situation, the children sit around the table while their mother decides how to spend the family money, they are being given a responsibility they are not ready for. They are not able to deal with the total picture as she must. They need the reassurance now, of all times, that an adult is truly in charge. Again, don't use the word *because* when discussing money with your children. If there is a disagreement, you should simply state that a certain expense is not in the budget. If fighting is necessary, fight the budget. Don't fight people—don't fight your children! Let them know that you are confidently in control of the situation; they will do better for it.

A Mother Is a Mother Is a Mother

Louise was so frightened about money, after they had filed for divorce, that she began to wince every time she heard the refrigerator door being opened. In no time she found herself screaming at her children about every little extravagance: too much shampoo, overuse of the telephone, lights carelessly left on. She had failed to create a detailed budget, showing on paper exactly where she was spending her income. Soon her children avoided coming home—it was no longer a home because she had not taken time to do her *homework*. When she did, she found that there was room in her budget for small errors and for an extra cookie at bedtime too. If there had not been a margin of this sort, she would still have been in better shape after researching it. She could have told her children calmly that certain things were not permissible, instead of screaming about it. This is not to say that children should be allowed to charge unrestricted through the refrigerator or to indulge as a general rule in energy-wasting behavior. It *is* to say that you will do a better job of guiding your children if you know what the facts are, and if you set a good example yourself.

The little things can be very difficult, with children, during this period partly because you are also worrying about much larger matters. What about private school, for example? Patty's children had always attended the local academy, and after school they had gone to the country club to swim and be with their friends. This was their way of life. Their concerned mother did not want it changed now.

Patty spent very little time pacing the floor over this question. Instead, she had a careful look at the budget, she decided that she would prefer private school to other benefits, and she left in money for tuition while taking out the sum she had wanted to set aside for the country club. When you make this kind of decision involving your children, you are making a very effective statement to them about your own values. You are letting them know what you consider necessities and what merely luxuries. They will learn from this far more than you could ever teach them by giving them everything. Patty's children turned out very well, by the way. And, in the meantime one of them got a job as a lifeguard after school at the country-club pool.

The mother who is a mother and nothing much else will be challenged now as she has never been before. Believe me, it will be better for her children in the long term if she handles it well. One woman I know about had great trouble in urging her eldest son out of the nest though he was twenty-five at the time of her divorce. The nest was too comfortable—he liked to sleep in it, and sit in front of the television set with a can of beer when he was awake. Martha took a good look at her financial future and decided this had to stop. She asked me how to convey to this outstandingly uncommunicative young man the thought that he should move on and take up his own financial responsibilities. She had mentioned the idea several times already, evidently without being heard. I made the following suggestion, which she carried out to the letter. I told her to bring home a collection of sturdy cardboard boxes and to begin putting his treasures into them. She was to say nothing but wait until he asked what was happening. When he asked, she was to say that she was helping him move. No further explanation. He got the idea. In very short order he was living with friends across town and working nights in a restaurant.

During The Interim, don't *say* very much, unless you are talking with your trusted counselors, dealing with the dumping of your emotional overload, and brainstorming with them about your future plans. I am not interested in what you *say* now but in what you *do*. And I am interested in what you don't say. One more *don't*—don't gossip. Watch out particularly for the telephone. It is easy to sit at the phone discussing all sorts of things that you have no business discussing at a time like this. Don't do it. Even when you are talking on the telephone with your attorney, watch your reactions very carefully. *Only when you see something in writing can you come to any binding decision.* You may have calls about legal and financial matters from your husband, from your attorney, from the accountant that will confuse you, frighten you, put you into a complete spin. Don't cry, don't laugh—ask to see it on paper. Say "Thank you very much for the information, and please put it into the mail for me." Much of your panic will be needless, to begin with; and then if there are ambiguities or questions remaining in your mind, you will be able to make a careful note of them *before* you try to respond. A great deal of time and energy can be saved in this way.

A New Will

A small but potentially important detail should be taken care of during The Interim: you need a new will. There are two basic items to be considered here, if you have children. One is the appointment of a guardian for their personal care. I recommend naming their father if this is reasonable; if totally out of the question, then name a friend (after first having obtained his or her consent, of course). The grandparents, we hope, will play a vital role in the upbringing of your children, but someone your own age should be caring for them on a daily basis. If you have the bad luck to choose a happy-looking family as guardians only to discover that they too were on the brink of divorce or other disaster, remember that your will can always be changed. This one is for today.

The second item is the appointment of a trustee for any money left to the children. Minors cannot own property or money, so you will need a responsible person to manage this part of their lives for them. Try to pick someone geographically near and financially knowledgeable. This individual should share your sense of values, as well, and have a real interest in the welfare of your children. If you choose wrongly, you can always change this later, too—but it is something you ought to do *now.*

Remember, when you are making your will, to write something down on paper before going to your attorney. *You* decide what you want done for those who are left behind after your death. Your attorney can't decide this for you. The role of the professional here is to write your requests in legal language so that there cannot be any misunderstanding in the future of what was intended. So, keep it simple and don't make a big, anxious deal out of it—but get it done.

The Interrogatories

The use of interrogatories and depositions is sometimes necessary in divorce. Sounds unpleasant, doesn't it? Well, it usually is. These are the expensive extras that come into play when the situation is especially complicated and/or when harassment of one party or another is a part of the picture. The interrogatories are lists of questions that must be answered in writing, under oath. Usually they have to do with the search for financial information that might be otherwise unavailable, but they can contain personal questions as well. Whether or not you want to send one of these, via the attorneys, to your former spouse is a question that should be calculated very carefully in terms of the cost-benefit ratio. In other words, find out how much the set of interrogatories itself is going to cost. Then figure out how much money you might uncover or reassign through such an operation (remembering that you are only going to get half, at most) and ask yourself whether it is worth it. The unexpected interrogatory arriving in the mail can be an unnecessarily savage blow, hardening attitudes that you might want to remain more flexible and pleasant during negotiation. This is sometimes a necessary step, but I never advise doing *anything* by way of deliberate hurt: nuisance, to me, has *no* value.

A client called me recently, halted in the midst of her job search by a forty-seven-page tome of interrogatories, containing no less than seventy-eight questions (most with subheadings) from her former husband's attorney. This intelligent professional woman of forty-two was in tears. Lucy thought she would have to call off all her job interviews and her career-counseling sessions for at least a month to answer questions having to do with literally thousands of pieces of financial paper from the distant past. She was an artist, not an accountant. At the same time, the interrogatories asked Lucy (who had raised six children) why she had not been working lately and why she had not yet found a job.

I was able to calm her down by explaining, first of all, that this was nothing personal. We are getting into the realm now of attorneys' devices, and sometimes attorney's "ploys." Lucy would not be required to do anything that was impossible for her to do. She could get an extension if necessary, and she could get help filling the forms out. She could apply "diligence" as required, without wrecking the structure of her own life at present, simply by remaining calm and purposeful and by transferring the burden of proof to the parties who requested it. She did not have to list all of her canceled checks for the past ten years and add them up in a dozen or more different categories.

All she had to do was answer honestly and briefly the questions she knew the answers to, then telephone her attorney for an appointment, with a list of the questions on which she needed help. Then, she had to gather all her financial records together and let the opposing attorney know that these would be available for inspection, by appointment. "Be my guest" should be her attitude. She should be gracious about it all, and undisturbed. If others want to hire an accountant to go through it all, that is their privilege. Ninety hours at fifty dollars an hour may be a little more than they want to pay. Lucy found that this interrogatory, rather more complex than some, took her only a few days' work after all. Meantime her attorney sent an almost identical one to "the other side" and it turned out that a great deal of information was uncovered on both sides that actually served to help Lucy's case. Remember, if you get an interrogatory, that it has probably been pulled from a file somewhere, and that only a few questions have been added that have anything directly to do with you. It's a habit of attorneys to pull off the front page, xerox the whole thing and send it back to the people on the other side: all very automatic, not pleasant but part of the game.

Depositions

You may, during The Interim, be called for a kind of questioning known as the taking of a *deposition.* This is done in a lawyer's office rather than a court of law. The purpose is usually to save time and court costs in the examination of a witness in person and under oath. Depositions relating to divorce can be designed to reveal facts about family finances, management of property, employment, children, and so forth, by way of gathering the information needed for settlement. Unfortunately, this is a device that can also be used for harassment, in an attempt to gain financial advantage by placing the witness in an uncomfortable situation. Don't assume that harassment is the motive if you are called for a deposition, but be on your guard.

A *good* attorney will take the time to advise the client patiently and carefully as to what the area of questioning is likely to be. He or she will explain what the client's rights are in refusing to answer or otherwise deal with malicious questions. The client will be told what the attorney can and cannot do by way of assisting during the questioning.

What are your choices? If you refuse to answer a slanted or a humiliating question, the judge will usually decide later whether or not it was necessary. If your case is being heard at that time in court, you will have the protection of that judge as to what is fair or unfair. Your only protection at the deposition is your own knowledge of the facts and the procedure, and the astuteness of the attorney you have retained. You can see now why it is so important to have good communication with your attorney, and solid trust!

In a way, you have already prepared for the possibility of a deposition: you have your records well in order by now, don't you? But you should also assume that you may be asked about your personal background from the point of view of employment, so prepare a resume of your experience as well, neatly and professionally presented. Include your educational background, job experience if any, volunteer work, church work, anything you have done for your community.

Have this on hand so that you may supply, if asked, all of this information in a concise form without having to reach back into your memory. It is important that your entire presence tell a story of confidence now, and of competence as well.

I have mentioned before that so-called no-fault divorce is the pattern now throughout most of the United States. More states are joining in this method even as this book is being written. I re-emphasize this concept, however, in connection with the deposition. Your attorney should advise you as to the rule in your own area (and let us hope that you live in one of the more enlightened states, where personal nastiness does not enter into this operation). In a no-fault state, you should not have to put up with any questions that are clearly designed to humiliate or to punish you. If the questioning is out of bounds, your attorney should object immediately. If you are in doubt, stop the proceedings yourself and ask to have a conference with your attorney. You do not know the law. You have hired someone to supply that information for you. Above all, tell the truth and then shut your mouth—don't ramble. Look on it as an interesting experience that will soon be over; do your best and then stand up tall and walk away.

All in all, The Interim is a time of what the attorneys call discovery. They are looking for papers, for facts, for records, for numbers, for logical positions from which to negotiate (or to argue) and you should be doing the best you can meantime to assist them. But you are also doing some discovery in other fields, inner places of your own. You are thinking of money in terms of what is really valuable to you. You are teaching these values to your children as fast as you get them sorted out, and you are doing that teaching, not so much by what you say as by what you do. You are discovering some talents you didn't know you had. You are dreaming of a future different from any you might have expected—and you are beginning to know how you might create reality out of at least some part of that fantasy.

We are going to dive into some murky technical matters in the next chapter, and I am going to do my best to make them entirely clear to you. But before we go on, read aloud to yourself the following statements. Try them on for size and see if they apply to you. If you're not ready yet, I hope that you soon will be. At this point, here is what *you* need to be able to say:

- I have now settled the question of where I will live in the *short,* foreseeable future.

- I know how much my living will cost, on a bare-bones budget.

- I have a tentative educational plan for myself and for my children.

- If those plans don't work, I shall change them, but they are a working start.

- And now, I promise myself to unload everything I have hoarded. The junky past gets junked now, and I will keep only the very best.

- I shall travel light and I shall learn to take some chances.

- I shall learn to balance my checkbook, to fix a leaky faucet, to change a tire myself.

- I shall continue to investigate my financial chances, learning what I can from professionals, but not dumping on them responsibility that should be mine.

- I shall find the best support groups for me, and I shall use them as needed while also helping myself.

• I shall be an adult around my children, and let them be children.

• I shall not be harassed and I shall not be intimidated.

• I shall not live with a condition that I don't like . . . except on a short-term basis for which there is a firm cut-off date.

Chapter 4

GETTING READY TO NEGOTIATE

WE HAVE SO FAR BEEN BUSY putting out fires. A little bit here and a little bit there has been done to control what has been essentially an emergency situation. We've had to deal with a difficult combination of numbers, papers, and emotions just when you weren't feeling like doing anything of the kind. Rest assured, though, that if you have made it this far in one piece, you'll be able to tackle the next job at hand.

It's time now to take a *thorough* look at every one of your financial assets: money, real estate, personal property—right down the list. You need to know exactly what is there in order to begin deciding what you are going to ask for in your settlement. The time you spend in *knowing* will be extremely important in terms of how well you are going to come out of this situation. You can get help from real estate sales people, brokers, insurance agents, and accountants, but the responsibility for understanding, making value judgments, and determining your selection is finally your own. And you are the one who is going to have to live with the decisions you make

To my mind, the perfect divorce settlement for a woman would be cold cash and plenty of it. If that were the outcome, you could then place that money in a variety of places, in investments tailored to match your new financial plan. But this is rarely possible. Most women have to accept something by way of settlement that they would not want to buy. Most will get less than we would ideally want for them. These facts make it all the more important that you should study your list of assets very carefully indeed, and begin to understand exactly what they are and how they can be put to work.

By this time you have made a list of all known family assets, and if you have any doubt about hidden items you have set your attorney to the task of discovering them. The first thing to do with this list now is to separate out any items that must remain the property of husband or wife. Items such as pension benefits, self-employment Keogh accounts, and Individual Retirement Accounts for each individual who earned these assets must be placed, in your new list, under that person's name. Even though these amounts are still considered "family moneys" they cannot be either divided or sold.

The Family Home

A home will very likely be the single item on your list with the greatest financial value. We have already mentioned the fact that this house of yours is more than a material object. Whether it is a tent, a trailer, a condominium, or a castle, it is a creation of yours that has brought you safety, peace of mind, and pride in its unique character, its beauty, and its hospitality. Now you must look at it without emotion, as a *thing* that very possibly ought to be sold. In case it is going to be sold, you need to know how much money it will bring in. If it is not going to be sold, you will need to know what your options would have been and why, from a purely financial point of view, it is more sensible to keep it. If your emotional attachment outweighs all financial considerations after all, then that is your decision. Fine. But you need to know what you are getting into and to do it with your eyes wide open.

If you don't agree with the local realtors' estimates, you may want to hire a certified appraiser who will give you an appraisal in writing, to be presented in court if necessary. Remember that the buying and selling of real estate is not an automatic matter. You can't assume that you will just put up a sign, that buyers will beat a path to your door, and that you will have a check for your asking price in hand after the thirty days of escrow. Financing of real estate often involves what is known as "creative selling," a subject we will explore in detail later. But if the price is right, if you are flexible in your approach, and use these creative methods as necessary, your house can almost certainly be sold.

Whether or not you are going to sell, you need to find out now everything you can about any mortgage upon the property. What is the rate of interest? Could this mortgage be transferred to another person? What is the condition of the house? If repairs are needed, could you refinance to obtain the necessary money? Would this be a good investment for the next few years? What is happening to real estate values in your neighborhood? Talk with people who know and get their opinions. Only when you have all this information *written down in your Financial Notebook* are you ready to begin making a decision as to whether or not you want to continue living for an indefinite period in this particular house. Warning: Very often I see cases in which a fine home is awarded to the woman in a divorce case but not enough money left to divide for her to keep it up. When you are thinking about trying to keep the house, assume that the chimney is going to develop a leak, that you are going to find termites everywhere you look six months from now, and that the cost of paint is going to go sky-high.

If you still want the house and can't see quite enough money in the till to support it, ask yourself "How would I feel about renting a part of it, or taking in boarders?" One client of mine, left with a large establishment and very little cash, rented rooms to students and found herself suddenly solvent, with built-in babysitters for her kids and a delightful new extended family to enjoy. Some financial advisers might have counseled her not to do this, but I said more power to her. What looks good on paper does not always provide happy living, and that is what this woman had achieved.

Real but Unimproved

In some portfolios we find investments in what is known as unimproved property. Basically, this refers to acreage with few roads, no utilities readily accessible, usually bought as a long-term investment with the expectation that its value will increase. Sometimes such land can be leased—for example, for grazing. But it is fair to say that such property is a luxury item and that it would rarely fit into the investment plan of a single woman. Most individual investors do not have the know-how or the financial backing to develop this sort of property. Property taxes must be paid, even though no income is being realized from the land at present.

Still, if you have such an investment on your list of things that must be divided in the settlement, you will need to find out all you can about it. What are the zoning laws in that area? Are changes expected in the near future, either in these laws or in the potential for development? Is anyone interested in buying this property? Could you safely keep this asset despite its current costs while waiting for the expected increase in market value? Give some time to investigation here so you will have an accurate idea of what the property is worth in hard figures. Then you will know whether or not you want it to be a part of your settlement.

Rental Units

Another kind of property you might own is a rental unit or apartment house. Investigation of the details on such property does get a bit complicated, but you make a good beginning by consulting your past income tax statements. Find the section on income property and have a good look at it. You should see there the amount of income received from rents. You should also find the amount of taxes, insurance premiums paid, maintenance costs, and then the most interesting feature of such property: the depreciation schedule. Depreciation refers to the amount of deterioration-through-use, a noncash bookkeeping entry. This is one of various items that will determine the amount of taxes you would have to pay if you were to sell the property. *Do not accept any property as a settlement without knowing what you are getting into, by way of taxes.*

It is quite common to find more than one mortgage on this sort of property, so be sure to make a thorough search on this point. You will need to know the total unpaid balance and interest rates involved. You may note that, according to your past income tax statements, this property shows a loss rather than a profit. This is quite normal business practice today. If the situation is complicated you may have to hire an accountant to help you, but you will probably find in any case that rental property is a wise investment only for those who have a high current income to count on. If the rents do not cover the costs, you might find yourself spending some of your support income paying those bills. You will also have to ask yourself whether or not you would be able to collect rents, see to maintenance of the building, and see that it is rented to desirable tenants.

Question: Has there been recent talk about rent control where the rental is located? Would that control affect your investment?

The most important feature of income property such as this is management. Hiring others to take the responsibility rarely works. The payment for their services generally consumes the profit you are seeking. Is the future profit worth your time? Are you willing and able to do this work yourself? If so, and if you have sufficient income to make a go of it, try to keep it. Many women have shown that this sort of enterprise is profitable when they can manage the details themselves.

Industrial Rental Property

Today many people feel that the very best of real estate investment is the ownership of industrial property—warehouses, small factories, even part ownership of shopping centers or industrial parks. There are real estate professionals who deal only in this sort of holding, and these people can be found by consulting a local realtor. Be sure that you are not seeking this information from one who is not an expert in the field.

On industrial rental property the leases are generally for a long period, perhaps two to five years, and a schedule of rent increases is usually built into the lease. Have the professional explain the terms of the lease to you, and note whether the renter maintains the property, whether he pays the taxes and/or the insurance. Your past income tax returns will be helpful here in telling you what kind of income is involved, and the amount of estimated expenses. When you have all this information together you will be in a position to begin asking yourself whether or not this property should be a part of your settlement.

Partnerships

Do you own any real estate in partnership with someone else? The question to be answered here by you (and only by you) is: Would I be comfortable working with these people—especially if my former husband is one of the partners? Find out the usual details about this investment. Does it require money from me for running expenses? Does it pay any income now? Is it possible for me to sell my interest at present? How are the market conditions? To whom would I sell? Would it be possible for the other partners to buy my portion? Get the answers to all these questions, find out as much as you can about the future prospects of this investment, and write it all down in your Financial Notebook.

Real Estate Limited Trusts

The real estate limited trust is known as a security. You may be an individual among many who together own many large pieces of property that are managed by a general partner. In this case, you must find out when the property was purchased, for the duration of this kind of an asset is generally seven to ten years. What has been its history of earnings? Do you receive any spendable money from this source? Once more, your income tax statement could show you the details.

One unfortunate thing about limited trusts is that, if you want your money before the trust is liquidated (all the property sold), you will find no one available to sell your share; there are no brokers who undertake this kind of business. So, this is not a liquid asset—not easy to turn into actual cash. The features of this sort of investment usually fit the high-income family, not the divorced woman who needs immediate income from her property. Thus you may want to use ownership of this kind as a bargaining point rather than actually plan to keep it.

The Farmer's Wife

The farmer's wife is in a tough spot when it comes to divorce. If this is a working farm and you live on that farm, you are going to have a very difficult time getting a fair settlement, just because of the nature of the situation. Certainly the value is partly in the land and the stock, the equipment; but the real worth of farm property is found in the individuals who manage and work on that farm. Often the property has been in the family for a long period of time, and it is not going to be sold on account of a divorce. Your number-one consideration here will be to avoid doing anything that will harm the working productivity of this property. Keep in mind that your financial future and possibly the future of your children will depend on the successful operation of the farm.

The farmer's wife will need an attorney who is familiar with agricultural property and how it works. I would also recommend an accountant in this situation, because you are going to need verifiable figures both on the value of the land and the equipment and on the crop values in the past. Your attorney may be able to work out a schedule of payment to you representing your fair share of all that has gone into that farm, but you should know that this may or may not be paid, according to the nature of events: drought and flood or a fall in the market can change the picture radically. Yes, money can be borrowed in order to pay you, in some instances, but this too is tricky, so get the attorney who is an expert in this particular area and rely heavily in this situation on professional help.

Second Homes

Do you own a cabin by a lake or by the seashore or in the mountains? Do you own a part of a house, or possibly a condominium at a ski resort? How much was paid for it? When? What can you find out about its present value? Sometimes vacation property is very hard to appraise. The current economic climate often determines whether or not there is an active market for it. It's a fact that fewer people go skiing and lie on the beach in Hawaii during a recession. Go to the local real estate people and get some estimates. Be sure you understand the terms of a partnership if one exists. Do you think the other partners would be able to buy out your interest if you did not want to keep it? Would they want to? How much would you be likely to get for it? What are the costs of maintaining this property? Be sure to include taxes, insurance, repairs. Know what your costs would be if you kept this asset.

Don't think "Oh, but we had such a good time there!" Or make up your mind that you're going to think about that some other day, not now. We're not dealing with an emotional situation at the moment—we're dealing with a piece of real estate. *"But I want my children to be able to enjoy it."* They don't have to spend summers at Lake Twinkletoes in order to survive. Can you really afford the luxury of a vacation home at this point? Most divorced people cannot. You will not be doing your children a favor in teaching them, by example, that it is perfectly okay to live above one's income.

"But it is highly desirable property!" All right, maybe you can rent it part time and obtain sufficient income to pay your costs. But be sure, before you go after this property, that its future expenses are not going to represent an unbearable strain on you, one out of all proportion to the expected benefits. Again, only pencil and paper will prove whether or not this luxury can be afforded.

The Mysterious Stock Market

If you already know all there is to know about the stock market, you may want to skip this section. I have been involved with it myself for years, and I still find it fascinating. But to many of the women I counsel, stocks and bonds are the most frightening assets they have to deal with. Often, the husband and his broker have made all the decisions and my client comes to me and says, "I know nothing at all about stocks, and they scare me to death."

All right, let's give it a try. First of all, a common stock represents ownership in a company. As partial owner, you share in the earnings and in the opportunity for growth of your company. This means that you may receive dividends and you also have the possibility of seeing your shares of ownership increase in value. The questions you should be asking are usually found in an annual or semiannual report from that company. It is probably being mailed either to your home or to your husband's place of business. Make a point of obtaining the latest report and reading it. Find out what the company produces and what it projects as its future. Don't get bogged down with all the figures, just get a general sense of what is going on. You can always go later to the broker who helped to make the purchases and ask some further questions.

Now have a look at *The Wall Street Journal.* Suppose you have some American Telephone & Telegraph stock in the family portfolio. Look at "AT&T" under the heading of "NYSE—Composite Transaction" (NYSE means New York Stock Exchange). It may say something like this:

ATT 59⅛ 45 5 9.5 7 4702 53 52¾ 52⅞ −⅜

Taking it from left to right, the 59⅛ means that is the highest price shares were sold for during the last fifty-two weeks. The 45 means the lowest price during the same period. The next figure, 5, is the number of dollars of the expected yearly dividend to be paid. The 9.5 is the percent yield on your investment at today's price.

The 7 means that the stock is selling at seven times its earnings. The 4702 (with two zeros added, making it 470,200) is the number of shares sold that day, and the 53 is the high price for the day. 52¾ is the lowest price for the day. 52⅞ is the "close" or the price per share you would use to figure the actual worth of each share you own. The minus ⅜ means that the stock fell in price ⅜ or 37½¢ per share.

This information tells you that today's price is not the high price over the past year, which suggests that this stock may have the potential of increasing in value. It says that it is not the lowest price of the year, if you are looking at it in terms of bargains. The five dollars per share estimated dividend yields 9.5 percent on your investment. A price-earnings ratio of seven to one indicates that its current price is average for this kind of company today. The number of shares sold that day, 470,200 is known as the "trading volume."

Learning to read the quotations doesn't make you an expert, of course. But it will give you a beginning, and it will make you familiar enough with the terminology so that you can show intelligent interest and ask good questions when you go to talk with a broker. Before you do that, by the way, you should also try to find out what you can about the companies in which the family does own stock. Some you will easily recognize, and you can follow the news of their progress in the financial pages. With the help of a responsible broker you can then learn what you need to know about the outlook for this company.

Brokers come in all shapes and sizes, Goods and Bads—and the bad ones are very bad! Don't let yourself succumb to the temptation of dealing with a friend. Seek this information only from a reliable brokerage company. You may have heard of the major companies in your area by now. Check with a friend who has had good communication with her own broker; this is probably the best recommendation. Make up your mind that you are going in with a list of thoughtful questions and that you are going to take notes on the answers. Ask for reading material and study it thoroughly when it is provided. Learn what you can about the product of each company you are involved with. None of this will make you into a canny trader overnight, and you aren't going to be buying and selling stocks very frequently unless you do become a real expert yourself. Still, it will pay you well to know as much as possible about the subject if securities are going to be a part of your personal future.

Whatever you do, don't jump the gun in your expectations about your stock portfolio. I remember a client who called me in a great state of excitement early one morning. She had doubled her money! "Well," I told her, "that is something I have a lot of trouble doing— how did you manage?" In a confidential tone of voice Gertrude assured me that the stock she owned was about to be split; for each share she already owned she was going to be issued another share. How about that for making money fast?

How could I go about advising the lady that "it ain't necessarily so"? The assets of her company were one pie, or one stew in a pot. When the board of directors decides on a stock split, the wedges just get smaller and the helpings less. A stock split may not make you money in the stock market. Usually it just means that the company wants to have more investors and has recognized the fact that more people like to buy ten shares at $10 per share than one share at $100. The lower the price, the more buyers is the hope. So be sure to get your facts straight before you start deciding how you are going to spend all that "magic money." More often than not, magic money simply doesn't exist.

One more warning on stocks. Remember that *all* brokers, both the Goods and the Bads, make their living on buying and selling. They don't earn money educating their prospects. So when you ask for information, keep in mind that this professional will be bound to have some desire to buy and/or sell something for you. There may be considerable eagerness on this subject. Do seek help, but make it clear that you will not be making major changes for some time. Yes, the broker is welcome to call you and give counsel, for you *are* now a prospect. You may want to call in yourself with a specific question: What is the prospect for this particular company in the next six months? Do you think they will increase the dividend? Just how secure is that dividend? But you are not going to begin playing the horses until you have learned a lot more about it; you are in no position to take up a career as a gambler now!

Bonds

In the simplest terms, a bond is evidence that you have lent your money to a corporation for a period of time at a fixed rate of interest. If you have bonds, you will want to know what the amount of that interest is. You will want to know what, if you sold it today, the going price would be. How long will the bond run until its date of maturity? What was paid for the bond when it was purchased? What is its quality?

There are those, such as Standard and Poors, which research companies borrowing money by selling their services. These research companies rate these bonds as to the ability of the company to pay the stated interest and whether they will be able to pay off the loan at the time the principal payment is due. These ratings start from a very highest quality, safety, and payout of AAA to a low of Baa and then a very few even lower. Because of the risk of not being paid back, the lower the rating of a bond the higher the interest. If one is going to accept a certain amount of risk, then one wants more earnings.

Let us again read *The Wall Street Journal,* this time under the listing for bonds. Good old AT&T will be here again, so let's look for that one. Perhaps you will see something like this:

2¾ 82 3.0 1 91⅞ 91⅞ 91⅞

This series of figures means: the percent interest promised on the old bond is 2¾ and the date when AT&T will pay the entire amount of the bond (which is $1,000) will be 1982. With today's price of 918.75, the current yield is 3 percent. If you own this bond, you will hold it for the next year and receive from AT&T one thousand dollars. The information you will need to make sense of your ownership is the price you originally paid for this bond. You might find old records on hand, or you could get this information from the brokerage company that was used at the time. *Remember that all investments have a cost price. Somehow or other you will have to get that information if it is not easily available within your own family financial records.* Look for bond certificates first, for they will show the amount of money that will be paid, and the name of the corporation that has borrowed money from you. It will also state the interest that corporation will pay to the lender for the period of time stated on that bond. It does *not* show, however, how much money was paid for that bond. For that you will have to consult your old financial records or the professional who facilitated the transaction.

Many people, while working through the contents of the family safe-deposit box, find some old Government Savings Bonds in small denominations, known as Series E. These may have been purchased as a patriotic gesture in the past, possibly as a part of a payroll deduction plan. These E bonds earn a very modest rate of interest, and so, if you find a large amount of money in them and if they have been held for a long time, you should check with a local bank to find out just how much interest they have earned. If you keep them, you may wish to convert these bonds into H bonds, which pay interest twice a year. No income tax will be charged on the past earned accumulated interest when this particular conversion takes place. At the time when the H bonds are sold, taxes will be due on the postponed amount from the old E series. (If you have the old Series E Bonds, some could now be forty years old and should be replaced with the current Series EE Bonds which as of November 1, 1980, paid 8 percent interest; the new HH Bonds paid 7.5 percent.)

Margin Investing

While we are talking about securities (which include both stocks and bonds), let's take a moment on the subject of the so-called margin account. You may find that your husband has been doing business on this basis—that is, borrowing money from his broker to buy stocks and bonds, and paying interest on that loan. A number of investors in the higher income brackets do this as a matter of course. It is legal to borrow up to 50 percent of the value of the purchase price, and you will need to know whether or not something like this has been done. The point is that the stock listed may not be entirely owned by you and your husband. The amount borrowed plus the interest due on that loan will reduce the face value of your investment. Find out from your family broker what the story is. Then reduce the actual value of these securities by the amount owed, when you are figuring actual value. Ask your broker to mail you a copy of the family monthly brokerage statement.

Mutual Funds

Mutual funds, anyone? A mutual fund is an investment company that combines the money of many investors into one large pool. This money is then invested in securities and is managed by the professionals. Each fund has an objective—which can be producing current income or seeking future growth in the value of your shares. Today one can find mutual funds that invest in the most conservative of companies or funds seeking profits by means of speculative ventures.

The latest addition to this field has been the so-called money market funds. These companies invest in short-term (thirty days to six months) certificates of deposit on a large scale and in government borrowings and foreign money situations as well, all this with the objective of earning the highest possible rate of interest at the time. They have an added feature that allows their shareholders to use this investment as a checking account, writing checks in amounts of $500 or more. There are no penalties for early withdrawal on these accounts, so you are offered a great deal of flexibility here.

The value of your mutual funds can be found in the financial pages of your local newspaper or in *The Wall Street Journal,* using the same method of interpretation that you learned for ordinary stocks. Just look under MUTUAL FUNDS. To find out how well your own fund is doing, go to the library and look up the latest information in a book called *The Weisenberger Mutual Fund Reports.* Here you can also learn more in detail about the composition of your fund. If it is doing well, you can count one of its advantages as being that it needs no management on your part. You simply enjoy the dividends. Just make sure they are coming regularly, at a good rate, and from a reliable organization.

Trust Deeds

We go into the whole matter of real estate in great detail in the next chapter, but if you find that you have a trust deed among your family's investments, you are going to need to know some specific things on this subject right away. A trust deed is a document showing that you have lent your money to someone who used it to purchase real estate. You will want to find out the terms of this loan. How much interest are you going to be paid, and for how long? Are you receiving any of the principal with the interest payments? When is the principal going to be paid in full? What is the quality of this negotiation—what is the credit rating of the individual who borrowed your money? (Because of the privacy laws, which restrict credit information, you would need the services of a real estate company here, or better yet, a mortgage brokerage company.) What is the current unpaid balance on this trust deed, and is the interest now being paid the same as that being charged currently for new trust deeds?

If the stated interest rate is less than what is ordinarily being charged today, and if you are forced to sell, then you will have to accept less than the unpaid balance. On the other hand, if current interest is lower, then the price could be higher, so that the earned interest will be the same as today's.

In the field of trust deeds there are what are known as "firsts" and "seconds." If you have sold a property of yours, you may find that you hold a "second" in the form of an IOU from the buyer. In effect, this is a lien against the property, with the rate of interest and the time the loan is due determined by you. This sort of transaction comes about when, for example, the buyer of your former home does not have enough money for the 20 or 25 percent down payment that is usually asked. You, the seller, have lent that money in the form of a second trust deed.

There are mortgage brokers who do the research and provide the lender with the person who wishes to borrow for the purpose of buying real estate. These brokers sometimes guarantee the returns by offering to buy the trust deed from you in case the borrowers stop paying you back. Check it out thoroughly, if you have a first or second trust deed among your assets. Depending on its reliability and the interest rate situation, this may or may not be a wise investment for you to handle on your own.

Bank Accounts

"I don't even want to think about bank accounts," many women say to me. "The thought of all those papers and all those numbers makes me literally sick." They are not alone in this; they have many friends, both male *and* female, who feel like upchucking when it is time to balance the checkbook. I don't know that there are any statistics on the number of males versus the number of females who turn queasy and see spots at the very thought, but there is a cure for this illness! Breathe deeply and take it one step at a time. Right now, we are just going to look at a list of *all* bank accounts that you and/or your former husband may have had in your possession and begin thinking about what they really mean. If you have suspected that your husband may have put money away into accounts you don't know about, your attorney should already be hot on that trail. But don't indulge in too much wishful thinking on this score. There may have been money, yes. But it may already have been spent!

You may have checking accounts, joint and/or separate; you may have savings accounts or special thrift accounts, and you may have been a member of a credit union. Get those bankbooks and records together in one place and ask yourself what that money has been doing for you.

Your checking account may do better in another

bank from now on, one that gives you a more favorable deal on bank charges or other services. As for your savings accounts, I hope you aren't like dear old Aunt Effie who has piddling little amounts scattered around all over town. Aunt E was traumatized during the Depression and she still reacts irrationally to the sight of a dollar bill. She is so afraid of loss that she won't put more than $5,000 in any one place at a time. But with the Federal Depositors Insurance Corporation now guaranteeing your deposits up to $100,000 there is no need to scatter your savings. Keep it simple. Keep it in one fully insured spot, giving you the highest interest rates available. *Do not keep large amounts of money in the simple passbook account.* These pay far less interest than the deposits that have time limits placed upon your withdrawal. Investigate those at your local savings bank or savings and loan and look into the money funds for the possibility of higher interest. Make a chart for yourself showing the dates when you will need money for major expenditures: property taxes, insurance, vacations, and the like. Arrange your deposits so that your savings money can be earning the highest interest for you while waiting for withdrawal.

If you are still feeling ill over the idea of actually juggling all these funds back and forth on your own and facing the monthly statement from your checking account, don't panic: you know by this time that money is a kind of *stuff* that is supposed to be working for you, not a monster that is going to devour you—and you know that you can be in charge. If you need help at first, hire the temporary service of a bookkeeper. But don't lean—*learn.* Take over the books as soon as you possibly can yourself.

Commodities and Collectibles

Moving down toward the end of your assets list now, we need to know whether or not you have purchased such items as gold, silver, or precious gems as investments. If you own gold or silver coins, make a list of them and take them to a reputable dealer. The evaluation will cost you a fee, and the appraisal will be in writing. No dealer can make an accurate appraisal without seeing the coins in question. Some will come to your home by appointment if the quality is sufficient to warrant the trip. For a small hoard, it may be well worth the small risk to take them to a reliable dealer. Make sure the appraisal can be made while you *wait* and *watch.* Then return it to the safe-deposit box. Do not keep valuable coins or gems in your home, and don't haul them around either. It's just too dangerous. An exception, of course, is precious gems you are having appraised that day; they must actually be seen.

Careful thought must be given to the selection of the gem appraiser. Don't take them to Joe, who runs the nice little watch-repair casual-jewelry shop around the corner. Check the yellow pages of the telephone book for a member of Gemological Institute of America (GIA) for your appraiser. When you go, take a friend with you. Some cities may have top jewelry stores, such as Cartier's, available; if so, call them and ask whether or not they make appraisals, and if so what their fee is.

When we are talking about "collectibles" we are getting into a tricky area. People collect stamps, antiques, works of art, comic books, all sorts of objects, with the idea that they may be more valuable at some future date. If you have such items in your home, you should have proper insurance already, with a clause known as a *rider* to protect their value in case of loss. Check that out, and consider whether or not such a policy should be updated. If you need a new appraisal, understand that there is a difference between the replacement value of your collectibles and the value quoted by the broker/appraiser. Their "real" value is what someone else might pay you for them. That, of course, may not be their value to you personally, and it may be less than what it would cost you to replace them. The dealer gives you a lower price so that he could resell them or auction them off and have margin for a profit. The important thing here is for you to be consistent in your estimates; make up your mind whether they are going to reflect the replacement cost or the market value less the cost of selling—one or the other.

Vehicles

What is your car worth? You have probably heard of the "Blue Book" value of a car, which of course is the present listed market price for one of that type, as found in a book which is generally in the possession of the local car dealer. You can get a good idea of this price for yourself simply by checking your year and make in newspaper want ads. Then call more than one dealer to recheck your own estimate and perhaps make an average. Take into account the condition of your car. It will be worth less if battered. More, perhaps, if you have put custom work into it or have upgraded it in some way beyond the norm.

Do you own a boat? Again the local dealer may be the only one who can help you determine a value, but you should also check the want ads. If it is to be sold, find out what the commission would be. You will have to deduct that.

It is not as uncommon as it once was for several people to own an airplane together and to use it for business purposes as well as for pleasure. Again you will want to check with newspaper ads and the local dealers in trying to set a price. If there is more than one owner, you will have to go after a copy of their written agreement. Who maintains the plane? What are the arrangements for payment of costs, taxes, insurance? This will help you to consider the facts of present market value and the judgments you must make in case this item is going to be sold.

Note: Many times when we look at items such as boats, summer homes or airplanes, we are dealing with situations involving business use. You may need some expert tax advice if this is true in your case.

Privately Owned Businesses

How does one determine the value of a family business or professional partnership? The answer here is "Very carefully!" Many of the same principles we found in our difficulties over the settlement for the farmer's wife are involved here. The greatest value of the firm may be in the people who operate it. We are dealing here in terms of what is very properly known as good will—how the public *feels* about this company, this partnership, and about its products or services.

A noisy, disputed divorce can in itself be harmful to the reputation of a partnership. It can be demoralizing. No matter what your personal feelings may be, consider the fact that your income will be derived from that business or partnership if you and your children are going to receive support. Don't do or say anything that may thoughtlessly or unnecessarily cause harm. Handle this situation with your gloves on at all times. When we get to the chapter on negotiation, we will consider the whole matter of good will in greater depth, but you should be warned now that this is a delicate matter.

The value of the business or professional partnership may require the services of accountants even to estimate. Equipment is there, but it is not uncommon to find that there are few other hard assets except in the cases where a building has been bought. An architectural, medical, or accounting firm may have its own building, and in this case the portion owned by your husband is a part of family moneys. This *could* be a large part of the family assets; if so, it presents an interesting situation. The valuation of the building itself is not hard to determine and must be listed as one of your joint assets. But you can see that a forced sale of that portion of the building might not be desirable (or allowed by the court) because it is the place where your former husband practices his profession. When appraising the value of a professional situation, be very *flexible.* The figures may come in high or low, and there may be special circumstances to consider. Get the best professional help you can on this, and ask the guidance of your attorney on details of negotiation.

If you own stock in a small company that your husband has developed with others, you may find yourself in an interesting situation, too. A client of mine was part owner, along with her husband, several other men, and their wives, in a small business. They were the only shareholders. Because the company needed all of its profits for growth and further development, no dividends were paid and there was no intention to change that policy in the near future. Now, my client and her husband were in the process of divorce. What should happen to their shares of the stock? Since it had never been placed on the market, it was difficult to know what value should be placed upon it. Figures were available from the company accountant, showing the value of the land, the buildings, the equipment. But the real value of the company was in the group of people running the business.

In the divorce settlement, our client received one half of the shares of stock owned jointly by the husband and the wife. So far, so good. She knew she could expect no income—no dividends. Then the husband said he wanted to buy out those shares—but what price would she be advised to put on them? We looked at Sally's budget to find out whether she could afford the luxury of *not* selling. She needed current income, but she also realized that her stock might some day be worth a large sum of money. Looking at the profit-and-loss records and the tangible assets, then making allowances for future growth, we arrived at a price, understanding that it was still nothing much more than a number on a piece of paper. Sally made the decision then to devise a compromise plan of selling. A number of shares would be made available to her former husband to buy each year, the price to be predetermined but flexible. He would have first offer, and if he should be unable or unwilling to buy, then she would offer the same shares to others in the company; if they did not take up the offer, she would go to people outside. It was a complicated business and involved legal advice as to how long she must hold onto her stock before she would be permitted to offer it on the open market. Still, under the circumstances, it worked out rather well. As with professional partnerships, my advice to those dealing with small businesses is be flexible, be inventive, and go after good, professional help *before* you begin to negotiate.

Personal Possessions

Here's where we can really get into trouble. Personal possessions are a very private matter, heavily loaded with emotional content. Make up your mind that you are going to be calm and gracious about every item to be negotiated here, no matter what volcanic activity is going on under the surface. It will be hard to do, but you will find that this attitude pays off for you in the long run. I have seen couples spending a small fortune on attorneys' fees to go to court and argue over who gets which potted plant. I have seen the entire final process of a divorce simply bog down over the ownership of a boxful of photographs. Don't do it! Keep your priorities straight, and realize at every moment that you have a long future ahead of you. There will be other potted plants, and other pictures of the Aegean, or of the Grand Canyon. Don't let yourself play power games at this point over trifles.

There may be some items of considerable market value and they may have increased since you purchased them. If you have fine china, silver, crystal, or a wine cellar, for example, you will need to make a careful inventory. You will want to have a strong basis for the sort of gentle negotiation I have in mind. If you have a piano, expensive stereo equipment, furs, jewelry, and the like, list them and research their value—again, being consistent as to whether you are referring to current market value, purchase price, or replacement cost. If you have items that were gifts, remove them from your list and document the name of the giver. Talk about a sticky wicket: What about the fine jewelry your husband gave to you, paid for out of family funds? This is the sort of thing I mean when I say that it is very difficult to put an absolute value on many things. You may say that these were gifts, and he may say that they were investments. There is no infallible way of determining the truth. You must simply put such items to one side and try to settle the other things in your mind, then return to the ambiguous ones later. Often people do the most nitpicking when there are few other assets to be divided. All the money has been spent. Do you really want to go on and on now, worrying over the bare bones of the past? I advise you to find as many agreeable compromises as possible when the time comes to negotiate these items, and get on with your new life instead.

At the bottom of the pile will be things like ordinary household furnishings, sheets, pots and pans, his clothes and her clothes, the supplies of daily living.

Don't sweat over these. Make a "his" pile and a "her" pile and be done with it. One of my rules for a divorced woman is: Travel light. Keep that in mind, and be generous.

Extras ad lib

Your list may be complete now, but of course each divorce is different, so have one more careful look at your own situation before moving on. There are divorces involving a good deal of conflict about the separate property owned by one or the other partner at the time of marriage: not all couples start out broke and happy, intending to build their fortune together. Can you document any money or property you brought into the marriage? Are there records as to your husband's previous worth? You should try to track these down and have them on hand by way of proof in case there is any disagreement on this score. What about your individual debts? Did you help one another to pay previously contracted debts out of family money? If so, you will want these documents too. The more information you can bring forward, the better and truer picture you will have of the assets now remaining to be divided.

Remember that in most states, these assets only include those moneys earned, saved, and invested during the lifetime of this marriage. If one partner's separate property has been given as a gift to the other, that gift must have been clearly established.

Of course, many people do not understand the significance of their actions in commingling their accounts and investments during a marriage. If this has been the case, only rarely can that money be recovered on divorce. Charlie, for example, received an inheritance from his mother while he was married to Sue. That was fifteen years ago. In the meantime he began to invest the money, listing his investments in joint ownership with his wife. All of their tax statements listed joint ownership, and this was a person who clearly meant to share his own inheritance with his wife. Now they are getting a divorce. Charlie wants "his" money back. If the marriage had been briefer and the period of joint investment much shorter, he might have a chance for recovery. As it is, he is going to have to live with the fact that he *has* shared his inheritance, and so it belongs one-half to Sue.

Think of your individual situation before closing the books on this part of our work, and be sure it reflects your own reality. Are there, for example, royalties on artistic work not yet collected? Investments where the future is doubtful, so you have not really thought too much about them? What about such minor but potentially important issues as a membership in a club? Does it have anything to do with your husband's profession or business life? With yours? What will be the financial or social consequences of giving it up? Do you need to keep it—and if so, for what reason?

Everything we have discussed in this chapter, and anything you have managed to add to it that reflects your own situation will be an essential part of the negotiation process when it comes time for final settlement. Don't make a move until you have got all the research you need done and until you have done some very careful thinking about the values involved. Then it will be time to start shifting items back and forth from the "his" list to the "my" list to get some idea of what you want awarded to you.

The work you have been doing on all this part of the divorce process has been difficult. Some of it was hard to understand. Other parts of it were very stirring and unsettling from the emotional point of view. Try to take comfort in the fact that it is going to pay off for you, not only in terms of financial benefit but also in simplifying the remaining business at hand. You won't have to keep running back and forth looking for bits of information later if you've got it all together now. And just as important is the sense of clarity about your own past that you can gain from all this. When it's down on paper it's understandable in some very new ways. You look at it, and you are now ready to move. You're going to "lose" some money and some property in this transaction. Accept that fact. And consider another fact along with it: if you *really* want to move, you don't want to carry a lot of heavy burdens with you. Look at your lists and imagine yourself walking into the next party you go to, or into a business office full of strangers, wearing a gorgeous outfit and a new hairdo, and a button on your shoulder that reads HAVE SMILE—WILL TRAVEL.

Chapter 5

TO KEEP OR NOT TO KEEP THE FAMILY HOME

IF YOU ARE LIKE most women today, you have a lot to learn about real estate. No one ever expected mortgages, taxes, and deeds of trust to be your long suit. The issue of shelter is looming large right now, and you wonder how you are going to begin making decisions about it.

Not every divorcing woman has a family home to worry about, but let us assume here that this is the case, because it is a common situation and because it will give us a place to hang our hats while we talk about problems of real estate in general. Most of my clients, over the years, have found that the largest available asset was the home itself, and they have shown me that the disposition of this item was fraught with emotion. The woman I am fearful for is the one who hasn't explored her options. She makes her choice without understanding the consequences and finds out that she has made a mistake that could have been avoided. We're going to try to see that this does not happen to you.

You should begin by asking yourself some questions, with a pencil in your hand and a piece of paper in front of you. Here are some of the things you are going to need to know:

- If I keep the house, what will it cost me to live in it?

- Can I live as cheaply anywhere else?

- If I sell, will I have capital-gains taxes to pay? If so, how much would those taxes be?

- Can I postpone selling for at least five years?

- Do I actually want to live in this house (rather than taking it from "him")?

- Could I obtain another mortgage, if I want to own another home?

- Is my present mortgage interest lower than the current rates?

- How does my neighborhood look? Will it remain attractive?

- If I remodel, will I "overbuild" the neighborhood?

- Will the zoning laws allow me to make this house into a duplex if necessary? Can I rent part of it?

- Am I thinking about shelter here or am I thinking about making money?

- How important is this house to the safety and sanity of the family as a whole?

In this chapter I am going to argue with you on all sides of these questions (and others) and I play devil's advocate deliberately, at times. But it's your decision. No one else can make it for you. If you feel that there is so much emotional commitment to this home that all other values should take second place, more power to you. If you say "I'm keeping my home," then decide, come hell or high water, that is what you are going to do. I'll retreat if you have made this decision *after* doing your pencil-and-paper work. I'll agree with you *if* you know everything there is to know about this house. If you're not staying in it to spite anyone. If you intend to stay in it for a minimum of five years. If you are willing to give up as many other things as necessary to keep your home. If you would go to work or take a second job to keep on living in your home. If you would get out on a ladder and paint it, if necessary. If you know how much it will cost to keep up the grounds, to keep the roof mended, to pay the rising costs of utilities, and the like and you still think it's worth it. If you know all this and still say *yes* to the family home, okay. Just be sure that decisions have been made only after some honest thinking has been done, and after all the facts are in.

I have seen women struggling to keep the family home and keep on living in it for a lot of negative reasons. Let's have a look at some of them.

Staying in the Neighborhood

There is the question of "staying in the neighborhood." What do you really mean by that? Do you mean "staying in the *right* neighborhood?" Perhaps you'll say the children shouldn't be moved away from their friends. You may really mean you'd be embarrassed at having to move out of Country Club Estates at this point. You fought hard to get there—what will people think? You made it to the top of the hill; you don't want to move down. It would do something nasty to your pride. The woman who is getting a divorce must realize that *the situation has changed.* Accept that, prepare to move ahead with due caution, and you will be on the right track. The grand neighborhood may not be what you need—or even what you really want at this time in your life.

The Monument

Another negative reason for staying put in the old neighborhood, or in the old house, is what I call "polishing the monument." You have lived a number of years in this place, and it is filled with memories. Your sense of security is tied up in it. If you can't have your marriage, you want to have the same living room, the same fireplace, the same chintzes and bookshelves, the same kitchen stove. Above all, you don't want to *move.* You want, in other words, to sit there, and you are willing to spend your energies year after year dusting and polishing this monument to a marriage that is dead. That doesn't make sense. It will not give you any opportunity to grow. If you really feel this way, maybe you will want to make some compromises in terms of a five-year plan for change. You shouldn't move too quickly and be sorry afterward. But you must know what is motivating you and have another look at your options. The choice is *yours.*

One typical example of monument-polishing was the case of the middle-aged woman I'll call Paula, who was building the "dream house" with her architect husband when the marriage finally fell apart. (Often a couple will try to solve their deeper problems by investing in some new living arrangement that they can't really afford. *Then* things fall apart, and *then* the situation may become a real disaster.) Paula had been struggling for so long to help provide this house, which was going to be the answer to all their difficulties, that she couldn't let go of the dream when the time came to face hard facts. She was offered the unfinished home as her settlement and determined to complete the work on it herself. Deep down, she wanted to show her former mate that she could do it: she didn't need him.

But she did not have a realistic plan and there was a great deal of necessary labor that she *couldn't* do herself. The salary from her job would only cover current costs of living, and even if she did get a homeowner's loan to finish up, how was she going to pay the interest? We looked at her options. She might rent a room to someone who would work on finishing the house in his spare time—but I did not advise this. The promise of "spare time" work is very ambiguous, and it seldom fulfills the obligation. The cost of labor is the cost of labor. How is it to be paid? I told Paula that she could do it herself if she wanted to go to school and learn how to do the necessary work; she could do it if she increased her salary to cover the cost not only of the loan but of all needed materials as well. I encouraged her to go ahead and live the dream if she wanted to that much—to the exclusion of everything else. Finally we came to the conclusion, which I think was a wise one, that she would do better to put the house on the market in its unfinished condition. Women can do the impossible, yes. But only if that is what they really want to do—for *themselves.* A divorced or divorcing woman works for herself now, not for public opinion, and above all not for pride or for envy or for spite.

When you think about owning a home at this time in your life, realize that this may not be a necessity for you. Women in transition may actually do better for themselves when they are not anchored to a house, with its problems of upkeep and maintenance costs. Renting may be the answer for you, at present. It may *cost* less in every sense of the word. Of course you want a sense of security, and you don't like the idea of "pouring your money down the drain" instead of building an equity. Still, there are advantages to be seriously considered in at least temporary rental situations. We will go into those further, but first let's have a look at some of the positive aspects of keeping the family home.

A Sound Investment

Margery was one of the lucky ones. She did her research thoroughly, and then everything fell into place. Her "bare-bones budget" was sizable enough to include costs of running her house, maintaining it, and paying off the mortgage. The interest rate on her mortgage was low, for it had been taken out many years ago. Margery knew that, even in the 1980s it is hard for a single woman to obtain a new mortgage and she knew that interest rates on a new mortgage would be much higher than that on her existing one. She had made her plans to go to school near the old home and stay in that area for at least five years. She was able to accept the fact that she would be hard-pressed financially until she was able to work full time, and she did not expect any luxuries. She accepted the house as a major part of her settlement because it was a sound investment; she kept it up nicely while studying computer programming and came out of her divorce with a home *and* an interesting new job waiting for her. Eventually she rented her home and moved to another city to pursue her career at a higher level. It was still a good, solid investment because she had made her original moves with her eyes open and all the facts at her disposal; she had made a sensible plan and had stuck to it through the lean years with her eventual goal clearly in mind.

How can you tell whether your present home is a good investment? You can begin by comparing your present mortgage payments with the ones you would have to make if you bought something else. Here is a table that may help:

House Price	Monthly Payment		Annual Income
$55,000	$395	10%	$16,000
55,000	470	12%	19,000
55,000	530	14%	21,500
$85,000	$600	10%	$24,000
85,000	700	12%	28,000
85,000	800	14%	32,000

This shows what annual income you would need to obtain a conventional thirty-year mortgage on a house at today's interest rates, with a 20 percent down payment, assuming that you can't get that mortgage at all if you need to commit more than 30 percent of your annual income to paying it.

Ask yourself now whether your present home costs you less than this per month. Does it leave you with a higher percentage of your regular income to spend on other things or to invest? Look at the remaining balance owed on your present mortgage. This balance can be looked on as a solid asset or not, depending on the circumstances. If the balance is low, say under $25,000 on a mortgage taken out fifteen to twenty years ago, then you have already paid off most of the principal and the fact that the interest is low does not make so much difference one way or another. But, if the home has been purchased within the last ten years and still has rather a large balance at a low interest rate, look on this balance as an extra asset. You know too that you will have better luck selling the place, if that's what you decide to do, with such an attractive mortgage setup. Homes financed under this system are currently moving better on the market, since a buyer can assume your mortgage balance at your low interest rate.

Now consider the size of the home and its general condition. With the increasing costs of energy, more and more large homes will be too costly to heat. Realistically speaking, can you really manage this cost over the long term? When are you going to need a new roof, new plumbing, and rewiring? How much is that going to cost, and can you afford it? Again, ask yourself whether or not you would be prepared to share your space with one or more tenants in order to keep this home? That's one way to pay the heating bills and maintenance costs. There are pros and cons to be considered on this, however, if it's the move you want to make.

To Rent or Not to Rent

Jennifer decided that she would keep her fine old four-bedroom home, which cost her very little for mortgage payments at a good, low interest rate. She was working now and had almost enough to balance the budget already; she just needed about two hundred dollars more a month to swing it. She decided to rent out her son's room, now that he had flown the nest. It had its own bath and an outside entrance. What could be better?

Her friends told her "You won't like someone messing around in your kitchen," but Jennifer felt sure she could adjust. She found a nice young woman who needed a temporary place to stay and began to reorganize her life on a sharing basis. A month later she was furious at the invasions of her privacy, the unfairness of their arrangements about buying food, paying for utilities, cleaning up. No firm guidelines had been set at the beginning, and Jennifer had become an altogether unwilling Lady Bountiful. She sighed with relief when the young woman announced that she was leaving and decided not to rent again until she had her rules and regulations well worked out. Next time, she was ready to talk business with the new renter *before* settling down. She rearranged her cupboards and her refrigerator. She made listed costs such as heating, telephone, weekly food, and household supplies to be paid for jointly on a sliding scale. This time she found a woman of her own age who was very grateful to be able to live in the neighborhood and could afford nothing more; all their arrangements were clearly understood ahead of time, and it worked out very well. Jennifer has rented this room for more than five years now, very successfully indeed. She has changed her guidelines from time to time as the need arose, but she has not felt "used" again, and she has had the advantage of never being entirely alone in a house too large for her.

The Duplex

Another possibility is to make your large old home into a duplex. This will require some careful research, but it may turn out to be well worth it.

Suzanne had made up her mind that this was where she wanted to stay for a long time. A duplex might be the answer for her. *She got out her pencil and paper* and went to City Hall. "Who can advise me about the possibility of making my house into a duplex?" was her first question. First she needed to find out about the zoning laws. The area was specified as R2. Good! This meant that she could have two residences on that lot. Next she needed an architect to show her how the house could be most profitably and agreeably split. She went to one recommended by reliable friends, a member of the AIA, and showed him the rough sketches she herself had made. They discussed his fee and probable costs. By now, Suzanne was knowledgeable enough to politely insist on getting this financial material signed and in writing. She also made certain that her plans would not conflict with the local building codes.

A few weeks later the architect presented his drawings and specifications for the job, a time schedule, and estimated costs. Suzanne took these to her local bank and began negotiating for a loan. The powers that be, of course, were eager at this point to rewrite her entire mortgage, but Suzanne was too smart for that. She knew that interest rates had increased to 4 percent above those on her old loan, so what she wanted was either a second mortgage or a homeowner's loan (sometimes called a remodeling loan, sometimes a home repair loan). On these the interest is usually a little higher than on a regular mortgage, but presumably you are borrowing a much smaller amount. She was told that she would have to repay this entire amount, with interest, within ten years, which is standard practice. Suzanne began to take careful notes so that she would know ahead of time exactly where she was going to get every penny of the money she was borrowing.

After a great deal of figuring and visiting other local lending agencies for comparisons, she came to the conclusion that she could afford it. If she was able to get her estimated rent and if the unit wasn't vacant more than one month per year, she would break even and increase the value of her house. After ten years the loan would be entirely paid off and her rent income would represent spendable money. The house was in good condition and the neighborhood was solid. Suzanne decided to go ahead. The value of the house was going to be, in time, her Old-Age Pension. She found the contractor, got the building permits, and went ahead. There were some bumpy times—costs unavoidably above her best estimates, delays caused by weather, and so forth. But she had been cautious enough, and continued to watch her expenses carefully enough, that she was not hurt. She had made it. The adjustment of living with a tenant close by would be another hurdle—but by now, she felt, well worth it.

There are other positive reasons for keeping your house and other ways to manage it. Have a careful look at your *personal* options now, while we are talking about the finances of real estate. Above all, this house is not going to be an albatross around your neck. It's a reality that you are losing a great deal in the process of getting a divorce, but keep in mind at all times what it is you are gaining. The other side of the same coin is *freedom!*

Try Freedom

Mrs. M. had been married for thirty-five years when her situation fell apart. She was over sixty and she could have gone to pieces herself and spent the rest of her life sulking. She was left with a large house— much too large for her to manage on a limited income— and she wouldn't be able to obtain her Social Security for another two years. What would she do?

What she did was rent her house for a tidy sum and join the Peace Corps! Into the safe-deposit vault went her silver tea service, and into the locked garage went her prize antiques. Mrs. M. went to India at sixty-three, had a wonderful time, made new friends, learned new skills, enlarged her horizons, and came home to a bank account.

You may even want to rent (or sell) your large home and take something easy to manage on a rental basis for a while, yourself. Face the fact that today, renting is cheaper than owning. "It can't be," you say. "I am only paying $350 per month for my mortgage, and that includes my taxes. I'm sure if I went out to rent the same house, it would cost me double." And you are so right, but the true cost of housing must take into consideration the dollars you have invested (the equity) in that house, and what those dollars might be earning.

If you own a house that is worth $100,000 and the unpaid balance on your mortgage is down to $30,000, you have to consider just what that other $70,000 could be earning if invested at, say, 8 percent—$5,600 a year, or $466 a month. Another way to look at that investment would be that the value of your home may increase at 8 percent or more per year. Is this a reasonable expectation in your own case? Both of these ideas must be acknowledged and considered.

Take into account, too, the hidden costs of owning a home. What money could you be earning, what satisfactions in life might be available to you, in the hours you must spend maintaining your home and doing the paperwork on it? When the draperies wear out or the water pipes burst, would you rather be in an apartment complex with a maintenance department in charge of putting things right? How important is your garden to you? Could you be as happy with a few flowers and vegetables in pots on a balcony, and the added freedom to spend your time in other ways? Would you feel safer in a building with neighbors close by and perhaps even a security-guard system; or would that make you feel less rather than more independent? How about your pets? How much do you want to travel? Can you afford to? For the person who would prefer less responsibility, more mobility in the future, the person who will not be settling down for some time, renting would definitely be the choice. But if owning a home gives you peace of mind even with increasing costs, taxes, and maintenance, and if you can afford it, then so be it. Keep your home. The discipline of paying that mortgage every month is probably the best savings plan in existence. You know you will do without luxuries to make that payment. Just remember that where your treasure is, your heart had better be also.

How about Taxes?

You might be amazed at how many women come to me for help with financial decisions and then, when I try to talk with them about taxes, say "Oh, I don't want to deal with that. I'll just let the accountant figure it out." By the time the accountant gets the material to work on, it is already too late. Moves have been made without regard to tax advantage, and all he or she can do is add up the proceeds and subtract the bad news. It is not the accountant's job to tell you how to run your life. It is his or her job to put the results of your decisions into mathematical order. You may receive advice as to tax advantages or disadvantages from a skilled member of this profession, but these are not people who can wave a magic wand and undo what has already been done.

Now, I do *not* believe that financial decisions should always be based on the taxes one is going to be forced to pay. Far from it. There are a great many other values to be considered, and there is also much ignorance about the tax that is going to be due on any given transaction.

First, let's set the record straight on some of the basic issues involved here: What are your taxes going to be if you keep your home, or if you sell it? The very bottom line is that Uncle Sam wants a piece of any profit we make. *You do not pay any income tax on your settlement at the time when you receive it, because that money was already yours.* The cash, the stocks and bonds, the house or whatever is your share of the family assets all represent a simple transfer from one place to another of what was once jointly owned. Your spousal support is taxable, and you will have to pay the taxes on that. Back in the family record book somewhere is information about the amount of money you originally paid for that house, and the amount of money you spent improving it. When you sell it later, you are going to be taxed on the difference between that and the selling price: in other words, on any profit you have made. The market value of the house at the time of divorce has nothing to do with it. I trust you have got those old figures in your Financial Notebook by now, because you are going to need to take a very careful look at them.

There are ways (which we will discuss) of postponing your payment of taxes on the sale of real estate. There are ways of dividing your responsibility for these taxes. But throughout the years they will follow you, waiting for the moment when you show a profit on your original investment in the process of finally selling, and there is no way I know of to avoid that time of settlement.

Be sure you understand the differences between the two basic kinds of taxes we are talking about here. It isn't really very complicated, and it's important for you to have it straight. *Income taxes* are paid on earned income and things like dividends from investments. Spousal support, salary, rents, royalties, fees for services, and so forth are the basis for these regular taxes by the federal government and most states. *Capital gains taxes* are Uncle Sam's share of anything we make in the way of profit when we sell an asset: real estate, stocks, bonds. At present, the rule is that we will pay taxes on 40 percent of that profit if we have owned the asset for more than one year. Even though your own tax rate might be in the very highest brackets, the tax cannot be more than 28 percent of total profit. Congress has allowed this benefit because the goal of creating jobs and encouraging risks in new business is of overriding importance.

Tax: If You Sell

Taxes are highly political and subject to change. It is your responsibility to keep your eyes and ears open in case some new law changes the ground rules in your situation. At present, however, there are a number of tax advantages you should know about in connection with the sale of real estate.

First, if you sell your home and then, either eighteen months before or after the date of that sale, buy another home of the same value or higher, any profit from the sale of your home is taxed "later"—that is to say, the tax on that profit is postponed. When you retire, your income will not be so high, hence you will not be taxed at such a high rate. So, this represents a "tax break" for you as long as you keep buying a more expensive house than the one you had before, or one of the same price. Now, on the purchase of your replacement house, you do not have to reinvest the total amount of money received in the previous sale. You may finance your purchase in any way you choose. The payment of taxes on your profit is not triggered until you sell and then do not buy or buy something of lesser market value.

Because of this practice of postponing taxes, in many instances there are going to be taxes owed if you choose to sell your present home and buy something more modest. So if there is any thought of accepting the home and then selling it, you must go after the income tax statements for the years in the past when you may have sold and bought residences. I do not mean investment houses you may have owned. The point at issue here is your home, your place of residence. The tax law applies only to this. If you did not pay tax "back when," watch out. Find out exactly what you are going to owe by way of taxes in a future sale and have that firmly in mind when you begin to make your housing decisions.

A tax law that is rather new has to do with the sale of your home if you are over fifty-five. If you have lived at this residence for three of the last five years and you make a profit on that sale, $100,000 of it is not taxable. In most cases this will cover even the postponed taxes and the gain in the home you are now selling. There is no repurchase necessary in order to gain this advantage. The big number to remember is the age of fifty-five. If you are near this age and considering selling, it would certainly be advisable to rent or stay in the house for a few years, until you have had your fifty-fifth birthday. This exemption can only be used once in a lifetime, but don't miss it if it is due to you.

Here's another pleasant bit of news about the postponement of taxes on real estate profits. If the divorcing husband and wife own a principal residence as tenants by entirety (joint tenants) and if they *jointly* sell that residence, they can split the transaction and then each may buy another, less costly home. *Both can postpone taxes*. The new residence must be purchased within the eighteen-month period, either way. This means that you can each postpone taxes on the family home and any other homes you made a profit on previously. You can each buy another home up to 50 percent of the market value of your old home without having to pay at your present tax rate. Not only that, but when over fifty-five, both of you can have the $100,000 deductible too.

Remember, this only applies if you own the house *in joint tenancy* and while you still own it in this fashion. Read the fine print in every document you are dealing with from now on, and here's a real estate tax story to help remind you of why you are doing it.

Our old friends Gertrude and George were settling the final details of their divorce when income-tax time came. Technically speaking, they had been married during the past year, so they filed jointly. Gertrude called up to see about signing the tax returns and was told by her accountant and her attorney that she was going to do no such thing. There was a "sleeper" in the works that might never have been spotted if her accountant had not been very alert. The family home had been sold six months previously and Gertrude had purchased a condominium as a permanent home for herself. George was over fifty-five, so they could benefit from the $100,000 deduction. But they had made a very large profit indeed and the remainder of it had been postponed, so that it would now be charged entirely against Gertrude's purchase of her new home. This action would take away her future use of her $100,000 exemption and have given her additional taxes to pay on her own on a home that had belonged in the past to her and to George as marriage partners. All hell broke loose when this was explained to Gertrude, but we cannot blame the husband too much, for his accountant was undoubtedly pressing him with advice to do this all along: "Look here, you do want to save taxes, don't you?"

The tax statement was changed, splitting the transaction, allowing equal sharing of future taxes and the $100,000 tax deduction.

The Real Cost of Selling

Get out your pencil and paper and see what it is really going to cost you to sell your home. Find out what the commission is going to be (it may be as high as 6 percent) and take into account such other expenses as escrow costs, termite inspection, necessary repairs, and "sprucing up"; these figures may well run as high as 10 percent of your sale price. Then you will need to go back into your records and find out how much you put into improvements over the years. Let's hope those records were well kept! Here's what your notations are going to look like:

Home:	selling price	$100,000	
	cost of sale	7,000	
	original cost	35,000	
	improvements	7,000	
	Profit	51,000	
		40%	
		$20,400	taxable profit
If your overall tax % is 30%		$ 6,120	tax due

Split Transaction

The above will help you see what your tax is going to be like if you sell the house on your own. If you are joint tenants, you may split this transaction to obtain future benefits in terms of taxes for both husband and wife (Revenue Ruling 74–250 IRB), and this is how your figures could go:

		Total	Per spouse
Home:	selling price	$150,000	$75,000
	cost of sale	15,000	7,500
	less original	35,000	17,500
	less improvements	5,000	2,500
	Profit	95,000	47,500

Remember that you must add to that taxable profit any postponed profits from previous sales of homes. *Both* husband and wife may now purchase a home with a value of $75,000 and continue to postpone the taxes (until selling to buy a less expensive home or not repurchasing). At the time of the "final sale" *both* husband and wife can take advantage of that once-in-a-lifetime exemption of $100,000, providing they have lived in that residence for three out of the five past years and are 55 years old.

Bifurcation—A Possibility

By now you understand that you don't want to be like Suzy, who rushed ahead and sold her home right after divorce, thinking she was going to come out with a nice fistful of cash—and then found out that there were postponed taxes and selling costs that almost totally wiped her out. What are the alternatives? Well, one that may make sense for you is to set aside the house in your settlement and arrange for you and your former husband to continue to own it for a stated period of time before selling. You can arrange your future plans to fit family needs and possible tax advantages. For example, you might want to stay in the house until your children are finished at the local school. After this the house could be sold, the profits divided, and the tax postponed for both of you. If the house is eventually sold after one of you is fifty-five, under this arrangement you can benefit from that $100,000 nontaxable provision. True, you would have to maintain his investment during this period, but it might very well be worth it in order to achieve your other purposes.

The Decision to Sell

You've had a good look at the whole picture from every possible angle and you have decided to sell. What is the first thing you do now?

Go out onto the front walk and take a very good look at the house itself! What could you do to make it look better, that wouldn't cost you a fortune? A fresh coat of paint on the front door, some colorful little annuals massed beside the steps? Make your house an instant showplace in these simple ways. Walk into it as if you were a prospective buyer, and begin on the inside by getting rid of the junk. Call the Salvation Army or have a garage sale. The rooms will grow in size as you move out the furnishings. Paint any surfaces that look shabby to a critical eye. Put good-smelling leaves and flowers around the place, or arrange to bake bread when the real estate agent is showing it! (Sneaky but effective!) Look cheerful when a prospect comes but stay out of the way and let the agent do the talking.

I would choose a reliable realtor rather than trying to do this job myself; there are many pitfalls for the inexperienced in this business. Once you have made up your mind, call several realtors in your neighborhood who are well recommended, ask them for their estimates of your home's market value, explain your mortgage situation, and ask them how similar pieces of property are moving at present. When you are ready to list your property for sale, incidentally, you had better not be in a wishy-washy state of mind. If you offer it at a price and someone comes along with that amount wanting to buy, you can't back out or you are very likely to be sued.

It is part of the real estate agent's job to make certain that the prospective buyer is really qualified; that is, has the financial background to pay you what you are owed. If you try to sell your house yourself, this is likely to be the hardest part of the job. You will have to have a recent credit report on your buyer from a reliable local credit bureau before you go any further with this deal. Next you will have to get forms stating the terms of the sale, and these must be filled out very carefully. You must state at this time any shortcomings in the home, such as equipment in poor repair or structural hazards, or you will be in trouble later for "failure to disclose."

This filling out and signing of the preliminary papers is another place where the agent can help. The prospective buyer signs them along with you, and now an amount of money must be put by the buyer into an escrow account. Escrow means that a third party holds this money, showing that the buyer is in earnest, and sees that details such as the title insurance policy are tended to. There may be contingencies to the fulfillment of the offer; the buyer may have to obtain a loan or wait to complete the sale of his own home. If you are selling the house without an agent, you will have to go to the escrow company and ask exactly what its services are and what it charges. These may be the people who can help you best if you are doing it on your own.

Option to Buy

Your house is on the market, and it has been months since you have received any kind of an offer. What can you do?

It may be that present market conditions are simply unfavorable. Check again with the local real estate people and make certain that you are not badly overpriced or missing the action for some other reason equally obvious to everybody except you. If it's generally considered a temporary problem, one very good way of getting around it is to rent your house with an attached *option to buy.*

This means that you charge a certain number of dollars per month above the rental cost for the renter to have, in return, first privileges of actually buying the house. The terms of the lease option should be for at least one year, and you will definitely state the price at which you would then sell. The amount of the down payment and all other details of that sale should be thoroughly spelled out on paper so that there is no possibility of later misunderstanding. Have a real estate attorney check your option before presenting it.

There are a number of advantages to this sort of arrangement. You will have some cash coming in on a regular basis, perhaps $75 or $100 more than you would have had on a simple lease. The rules for the $100,000 tax forgiveness allow you to rent your home for two of the past five years and still collect that tax-free profit. You can wait for the market to strengthen before selling, and you can be pretty sure that your tenants will take good care of the place, because they are after all people who may want to own it themselves.

Creative Selling

Before leaving the subject of selling real estate, look at one more possibility—an important one. And when we discuss creative selling of your home, be thinking at the same time of creative buying. If you are going to sell your old home and then buy another, you may find that this information can work for you on both transactions.

One of the easiest ways to sell a home these days is to act as the lending agent yourself. In order to do this safely, you will have to know your own financial plans down to the penny. It means tying up funds of your own for a period of five to ten years, usually at an interest 1 percent lower than the current lending rates for real estate (but remember, those rates are apt to be high). Can you afford to invest this way, or do you need the cash to spend on more immediate necessities?

If a prospective buyer comes along who can afford to give you the amount you need in cash as a down payment, you might accept his IOU (a note for the balance due) secured by a first trust deed. Is there a risk? Yes, there is a risk in anything you do with money. Make sure the person's credit is good before you go ahead. Then, if payments are not made, you have the legal right to foreclose. You can go to court and arrange to have the person forced from your home. I wouldn't like to go through that process myself, but it is good to know that it is there for our protection.

If the buyer does not have the cash even for the down payment, in some circumstances you may want to lend even that. In this case you get what is known as a second trust deed. You lend up to 10 or 15 percent of the selling price on specified terms. There is no one way to write up these terms, so the seller and the buyer simply have to arrive at an arrangement acceptable to both. The duration of this note is rarely over five years, and it usually specifies that a certain amount of interest is to be paid for such a period and then the entire balance is due. The theory is that the buyer will come up with the cash by that time, perhaps by means of remortgaging the home itself.

If your present mortgage doesn't have a "due on sale" clause, you may be able to make it an attractive part of your financial package for a prospective buyer. The old, low-interest mortgage is obviously desirable— if you can arrange to have it transferred and if the buyer is qualified to undertake this loan. You will want to weigh this strategy against the tax advantages you might have if you retain ownership yourself meantime and continue to pay your own old mortgage. I don't believe in planning one's life around taxes, but it is wise to look at all the options before making these rather complicated decisions. If you sell, you will still have eighteen months in which to decide whether or not you are going to buy another home in order to qualify for tax postponement. You are not going to hang onto this house *simply* for tax advantages, and you are not going to run out and buy the first thing you see after selling this one *simply* for tax advantages. You're going to have all the options down on paper where you can see them instead, and then you're going to make a sensible, firm decision.

Financing Another Home

We're now thinking about buying as well as selling. Actually, real estate people keep track of couples who are talking about divorce! It's a little like ambulance-chasing, I suppose, but divorce brings business to the realtor. Usually the family home is sold, and there may very well be two more purchases in the works as a result. All of this produces commissions for the professional real estate person, as well as fees for the accountants and the attorneys.

Not long ago buying a home was a great deal simpler than it is today. You would call up the savings and loan people and ask their rate of interest on a home mortgage. A pleasant voice would give you a figure and invite you to come in and discuss things further. You would go to see this nice person and find out how many years the mortgage was going to last. You would probably be told twenty or thirty years. During this period you would be paying interest on the unpaid balance and finally would pay the last of the money you had borrowed, as well. This is called a conventional loan where the principal is amortized—paid off on a regular basis, along with the interest.

Due to fluctuation of interest rates in the last few years we now have a number of other ways to borrow money for the purchase of a home. Here is a list of them for you to consider:

> *Graduated-Payment Mortgage* On this one, there is a fixed rate of interest charged, but the monthly payments are lower during the first year and then gradually increase until the fifth year. At this point they level out and continue the same for the rest of the term of the mortgage. This method can lower your first-year payment by as much as 20 percent. The rate of interest will be a bit higher than in the conventional mortgage.

> *Pledged-Account Mortgage* In this one, the amount of the down payment is placed in an interest-earning savings account. During the first years of the mortgage, regular withdrawals are made from the account to add to the low monthly payment on the mortgage. The interest rate will be higher than on the conventional mortgage.

> *Variable-Rate Mortgage* The interest rate here can vary within predetermined limits of, say,

2½ percent according to a "cost of money" index: the Federal Home Loan Bank Board. Changes in the interest rates can be accompanied by changes in the monthly payment as well, and/ or in the number of payments you are to make. Possibly you will find here a stipulation that there will be no prepayment penalty or an open line of credit at the going mortgage rate.

Roll-Over Mortgage The interest rate is renegotiated every five years or so. The reference index is the current market rate for new mortgages on previously occupied homes. Maximum rate increase or decrease will be about ½ percent per year and 5 percent over the life of the entire mortgage, which is usually thirty years.

Flexible-Payment Mortgage This one calls for interest-only payments over the first five years. After this time, payments must be fully amortizing, meaning that they must be paying off both interest and principal.

Wraparound Mortgage When the seller is also going to be a partial lender, there is something called a wraparound mortgage. The seller, who now has a very attractive low-interest mortgage, accepts a 15 or 20 percent down payment in cash, continues to pay the payments on the old mortgage, and accepts a second trust deed for the balance owed. He would offer the buyer an interest rate on the total unpaid balance of the purchase price—less the down payment—at a rate less than the prevailing rates. This would mean that the seller would make added interest above what he is paying his lender, and the buyer could lessen his interest cost rather than going to a lending agency. In some areas, even the lending agencies are offering this kind of financing. Is there risk to the seller? There is always risk when dealing directly with another individual, but it could be a calculated risk, one that could be acceptable if the credit of the individual was good.

All these methods are ways of responding to the needs of people who want to purchase homes but have little cash to put down. They may be forced to borrow more than the usual 80 percent of the purchase price, a definite disadvantage because of high interest rates. On the other hand, if they wait until their down payment can be increased, what will be the increased cost of housing by that time?

A final note on buying another home: There are some loans for this purpose being offered at 8 or 9 percent interest ("appreciation-participation loans"), but watch out for these. The catch is that when you sell the house later on, your lender is going to share in the profit. This method may offer you shelter at the only price you can afford, but your future is an unknown quantity right now, and we want to build up as much security as possible for you.

For one thing, you are going to live until you are at least eighty years old—remember? (And that figure may have gone up to ninety or one hundred since I began writing this book.) Times are changing fast, particularly in relation to the elderly. The woman who once would have signed herself up for "lifetime care" after a midlife divorce is nowhere to be seen. She's off to the South of Spain instead, or out learning to disco. She's taking courses in Japanese, in medieval philosophy, in television editing. She's also beginning to make some money these days for herself, buying and selling real estate.

Chapter 6

INSURANCE

THIS IS A VERY BRIEF chapter on insurance matters. Don't let them go any longer if you haven't already tended to them. This is a time in your life when you want all the financial safety you can negotiate at a price you are able to afford.

What is insurance, really? It's a plan for replacement of a loss, but even more basically it is a method of sharing the cost of a catastrophe. By keeping records of how many fenders get smashed, the auto insurance company can charge a small fee to a great many people; they can then pay for the fenders that are actually in the accidents and also make a profit for themselves. Years ago, when the farmer's barn burned, the neighbors all came to the rescue and built him another one. Today we have insurance companies who do that for the community by collecting from everyone to help pay for the person in trouble.

A human being certainly cannot be replaced, but that person's future income can be replaced by life insurance. Statistics tell the insurance people how many individuals will die this year and at what age. The cost of the life-insurance premium is calculated to pay that many death benefits and also allow a profit to the industry.

Now that you are on your own, it is your responsibility to find out what insurance coverage you need. The first that comes to mind is probably automobile insurance; we are all very much aware of the amount of damage these vehicles can do. If you were to have an accident and injured a person, or damaged his or her car, you could be sued. What you need to cover this possibility is a kind of insurance called public liability and property damage. The amount you should be covered for will depend on your own financial position and also upon your own state laws regarding minimum coverage.

You can extend coverage on your automobile to include repairs to your car if it is damaged in any way. Commonly this will involve a deductible clause, meaning that you will pay for things that can be repaired for $100 or $250 or even $500; the insurance company then pays for anything above that. You will want to have enough money on hand to pay for the deductible amount, because you are buying insurance to protect you from the real catastrophes.

Today, insurance companies often sell what is known as a package. This is a mixed bag of events to be covered. For example: hospital payments if someone is injured in an accident and cost of renting a car while the other is repaired. Items lost or stolen from the car may also be on this list. Public liability and property damage are an absolute must for you, but the others will be optional. Read the fine print and find out exactly what you are buying. If the cost is not too much, get as many added features as you can. A good way of deciding what company to work with is to ask your local auto mechanics what they know about the kind of cooperation their customers have had from which insurance outfits. You can telephone around and do some comparison shopping for insurance while you are at it.

Incidentally, you must be *very* careful during this period of your life—even more careful than usual—whenever you get behind the wheel of a car. Statistics show that people who have just been divorced (or widowed, or who have suffered some major loss recently) are much more likely to have accidents than the rest of the population. You obviously don't want anything like this to happen to yourself or anyone else to whom you might cause injury—but it's also a financial hazard at this point. Your insurance rates may soar if you start realigning your fenders by mistake.

Homeowners' Policies

Some kind of homeowner's insurance is another absolute necessity. You must have adequate fire insurance on your home. Be sure to look carefully at whatever policy you may have already, and get it updated if necessary to include coverage for the greatly increased costs of labor and materials for replacement.

Fire insurance has been packaged recently with a number of other types of coverage. Look for features offering replacement of items stolen or destroyed by vandalism. In some areas you will want to buy peace of mind by getting coverage for damages caused by earthquakes, floods, hurricanes, or tornados. Also, we have to recognize the fact that we live in a litigious society—one in which people in general are prone to sue at the drop of a hat. Your homeowner's insurance should contain a section on public liability, offering payment for any lawsuit against you on account of injuries sustained on your property.

If you have things of special value in your home, be sure to bring them to the attention of the insurance agent. Items above ordinary value will not be covered in your regular homeowner's policy, and you will want what is known as a rider to give you extra coverage. Take the time to make an inventory of everything in your house, and take photographs of everything, especially the most precious things you own. You may want to get a professional appraisal of your furnishings, particularly if you have valuable furniture, antiques, rugs, or fine art. Insurance companies are far more likely to accept a document provided by a licensed appraiser than they are to accept a homeowner's valuation when it comes to making settlement of an insurance claim. The cost is minimal compared to the benefits. Then store your list and the pictures in your safe-deposit box. In this way you are protecting yourself against loss that could not be proved in case of theft, fire, or other catastrophe. You may feel that this is a nuisance, but you will be glad you did it, whether or not trouble does strike. It is one of those simple things you can do for yourself that helps to give you a solid feeling of security.

Health Insurance

If you are not employed and covered for medical expenses by your employer, health insurance is hard to shop for. In addition to the terribly high costs of medical care today, there are many policies sold that are almost worthless.

If that can't be done, begin by doing some thinking about your individual financial situation. Ask yourself whether you can afford to handle your ordinary medical costs: physical exams, shots, and so forth. Now is the time to go back into your Financial Notebook to find out exactly what those costs have been in the past. If you can cover these, then you will probably want what is known as a major medical health insurance plan. This will begin covering your costs after a deductible as in auto insurance, the usual deduction being $500 or $1,000.

Be sure you are buying something realistic in terms of today's medical costs. A policy paying you $50 a day for a stay in the hospital doesn't make much sense if the bill is going to be closer to $200 per day. The average number of days in the hospital is seven; so don't buy a policy that doesn't start paying you until day five.

Remember that if you have read all the fine print and find you have still made a mistake on the insurance you've bought, you don't have to live with it. You can go after a better policy while the inadequate one is still in effect. Then you can cancel the other one as soon as you are covered properly.

When I work with women who are going to be raising the children after a divorce, I always have them ask that the father provide continuing health coverage; often he can do this rather simply through his own employment situation. If there is no protection available from that source, then we look for a local Health Maintenance Organization. An HMO will offer a prepaid plan that gives you almost unlimited care for a predetermined rate. This is often the best protection available for the least expenditure.

Life Insurance

Life insurance is a sticky subject, because it is not really about life. It is about death, and no one wants to think of that. But it is an important business, and it may be particularly crucial if you are depending on spousal and child support over a period of time. What is going to happen if the source of that income suddenly departs this life? You are not going to be in very good shape. Remember: the purpose of life insurance is to replace a wage-earner's future income.

If your husband is insured by a group insurance policy as an employment benefit, there can be a statement on your divorce decree that will continue to name your children as his beneficiaries. This should definitely be a part of your requests, at least until the children are over the age of support.

What about insuring your own future support? The first step would be to go back to your research about the amount of family coverage you already have, to insure your husband and the cost of those existing policies. Figure out just how much you think will be the amount of future alimony, based on your temporary support. Now, subtract any loans taken against your present policy from the face amount, and you will know how much you are due to receive in death benefits. Is this at least 50 percent of your expected future support? It should be. Now, determine how much you are paying for this per thousand dollars of death benefits (the face amount). You do this by dividing the total amount by the amount you pay on your premiums. It might be better for you to get a cheaper policy for the comparatively brief period in which you will be receiving spousal and child support, but you won't be able to shop wisely unless you know what you are really paying for your benefits at present.

Some insurance companies have combined "pure insurance" with various kinds of savings plans. These are known as cash-valued policies. Very often the luxury of that added savings account makes the cost of the death benefit too expensive for the woman who is on her own; also, it may be paying very low interest compared to other places where you might put money to use. But this is the reason why some insurance policies are said to have "cash values"—and the reason you should place this on your list of possible assets. Be certain, of course, before calculating the value of yours that you have taken into account any outstanding loans on this policy and any interest that must be paid on those loans.

We have explained that the so-called permanent cash-valued life insurance is a combination of a death benefit (pure insurance) and a savings account. The price of life insurance may be difficult to determine; for instance, New York Life Insurance Company has more than forty-eight different policies, all with different costs, all paying the *same death benefit.* These differences are determined as to the arrangement and conditions of the savings account.

Participating is another word that must be understood. *Participating* means that a dividend is paid, usually once a year. Normally when one hears the word *dividend* one thinks of earnings, but with life insurance dividends are actually a return of an overcharge. Hence the Internal Revenue Service doesn't charge you income tax on these dividends, for it has determined that they are not earnings. The true cost of the policy is actually your premium less expected dividends.

To determine whether the savings factor in your policy is a good investment, do some arithmetic to say "If I had my money in another earning position, say a money fund, a tax-free municipal bond fund, a bank time account, or other investment vehicle, would I do better?" Of course we must admit that some people who have a hard time saving money might have to have a discipline and the life insurance policy would offer this. The names of policies that have cash values could be whole life, ordinary life, straight life, and a multitude of fancy names.

You need to know now whether your husband could pass a physical examination, in case you want to try for another sort of policy. If he can, you may want to trade in the old cash-valued insurance for something called an annual renewable term, which may be as little as one quarter the expense of your present plan. You will want to check with your insurance agent on this. Don't give up that old policy until you have the new policy in your hand!

If your husband cannot pass a physical, then you

have to work with the existing policies. In this case, find out what the cash values are, then read further to find out what this would mean in "paid-up term insurance." If you can convert that insurance to paid-up term, and in some cases even pay off the existing loans against it, you may be much better protected at a lesser cost. When the period of support has ended, cancel the policies. Or you might graciously offer them back to your former spouse, for your need for them will no longer exist.

You should consider life insurance on yourself only if your future earnings are needed to support your children. If that is the case, then shop for the least expensive *term* insurance to cover that temporary need. Drop that insurance when your children are on their own. Don't forget, by the way, that you will be eligible for Social Security benefits as your husband's spouse if you have been married for more than ten years. Be sure to check with your local Social Security office to see exactly what those benefits will be and how to get them coming your way.

And don't forget that the very best insurance of all is *you.* Your health and peace of mind, your talent, your determination to take charge of your own life—these are forms of security that can't be bought. Back yourself up with what you obviously need, because it is worth spending money to keep yourself secure against the big disasters. But don't do it in a timid mood; and once it is done right, put those papers away in your Financial Notebook and prepare to get on with your life.

Chapter 7

NEGOTIATION

ONCE IN A BLUE MOON or so, a divorcing wife and husband agree immediately on the terms of the final settlement. When this happens, no negotiation is necessary. Almost certainly, however, you are going to have to dicker and compromise along the way, and this process may take weeks, months, a year, or even longer.

The judge will make the final decision if you, your husband, and your two attorneys simply cannot come to an agreement. I always hope this will not happen to my clients, because this trip to court involves expenditure of time, money, and energy that could be used elsewhere. If your attorneys have your best interests at heart, they will be urging both of you to be flexible and fair-minded. Some attorneys, however, enjoy an unnecessary fight for personal reasons, and others are not averse to piling up hours on a job such as this in order to increase their own charges. Watch out if you suspect that this may be happening. If your husband's attorney is one of these, there may not be very much you can do about it. If yours is, you may want to reconsider your commitment to him or her. Later in this chapter we will take up the question of changing attorneys; for now, we just mention the fact that it is always possible to do so.

Negotiation is an art understood only by high-level politicians and corporate businessmen—right? *Wrong.* You, as a woman, have been negotiating ever since you have been in kindergarten. Think back on the behavior of kids in the playground. When Tommy wants a turn with the big red wagon, more likely than not he beats Freddy over the head with a shovel to get it. Susie takes a look at the situation and figures out a way to make a trade instead. (This of course after she has been whacked over the head by a considerable number of shovels. Eventually it occurs to her that the boys are bigger than she is and that her head was meant for better things.)

The British military historian B. H. Liddell Hart has written an excellent statement on the art of negotiation. It will help you avoid the twin pitfalls of female negotiators: *giving up too soon* and *overkill.* I have seen depressed and frightened women throw up their hands and accept the first offer made to them just because they can't bear thinking about the situation. This, of course, can be a terrible mistake. On the other hand, women whose pride has been wounded in a divorce situation sometimes come out fighting brutally when tactics like these simply are not going to work. Your attorney is going to do most of the talking for you at this point, of course, but your attitude is all-important in guiding that professional. *Refusal to settle prematurely* and *willingness to settle when the time is ripe* ought to be your clearly understood goals. Here's what the military expert says about the negotiator's ideal attitude:

> Keep strong if possible. In any case, keep cool. Have unlimited patience. Never corner an opponent, and always

assist him to save his face. Put yourself in his shoes, so as to see things through his eyes. Avoid self-righteousness like the devil, for nothing is so self-blinding.

You might want to paste that up on your mirror and memorize it.

By this time you should have figured out (with the help of your attorney) exactly what assets are available to be divided. If you have suspected anything by way of funds or property has been hidden away, you have instituted a thorough search. You know your goals—what you will plead for, in court if necessary. You're aware that some items simply cannot be divided. These you have moved from one column to the other of your master list of assets in an objective attempt to arrive at a fair balance. Fair balance? Yes! You are not going out for revenge. You are not being unrealistic or emotional. You've studied the laws of your state and you have a reasonably good idea of what to expect.

In other words, you are going into the negotiation process thoroughly *informed.* You have made up your mind not to pay any attention to the horror stories you are bound to hear at this juncture. At no time are these stories helpful, but they tend to collect around a woman who is going through any of the traumatic events of life, whether it be childbirth, menopause, or divorce! Ignore them and carry on with your own rationality and dignity intact.

The First Offer

The first offer is probably going to come from the husband, simply because he has been the financial manager in most cases. By now your own first offer should be on paper and in your attorney's office with a photocopy in your own Financial Notebook. Should you be talking over the terms of these first offers directly with your former spouse? Check with your attorney. Usually it will be best to say nothing at all. If you do discuss any part of the final settlement with him directly, do it in very cautious terms. Be cool and speak with gentle objectivity, no matter how you may be feeling inside. Be sure not to mix your issues in any of these discussions: don't talk about money side by side with the matter of child custody. Don't mix trivia in with any major issue. In fact, avoid trivia altogether. Don't make the mistake of trying to hasten things.

The *only* reason for accepting the first offer is that it may be quite a generous one. If the husband is eager to switch partners, he may be feeling guilty and at the same time wanting to get things over with as soon as possible. That's his problem, not yours, but you may find it to your advantage to settle quickly in such a situation.

There are many divorces, however, in which the husband will have to be given a number of months in which to cool down and to realize that he is no longer completely in charge. If the first offer is a mean one, don't panic and don't fly into a rage. Your comment at this should be "That is very interesting." Period. Hold your fire! There are going to be many other proposals going back and forth between you in a case like this. You may have to teach him rather slowly that you are no longer going to take a submissive role. I have seen new respect dawning in the eyes of husbands who see their former wives in a completely new light during the process of divorce, when it is properly handled. It's worth a lot of waiting, a lot of self-education on your part to experience a moment like this!

See It in Writing

Don't let anyone—even your attorney—try to tell you about offers for settlement over the telephone. You are going to fly off the handle if you don't know what the facts really are. Get it in writing, read it over quietly and carefully, making notes. *Then* discuss it with your attorney. *Then* react.

You will want to check off the parts of the offer that may agree with your own proposal. Then narrow down the list of items for discussion to focus on what is unacceptable to you. What are the options? Where are the possibilities for compromise?

Taxes, Taxes, Taxes

Look very carefully at the tax problems associated with each item in the settlement. Are you perfectly clear in your own mind that the transfer of assets accumulated during this marriage represents *a confirmation in your name of what you already own?* This is why it is not taxable to you when it is transferred to your name alone. Tax laws recognize the fact that you are only getting what belongs to you anyway. You will pay income tax on these assets only at the time of their future sale. Spousal support, however, is regarded by the tax boards as income. They want a piece of that action as it occurs, and you will be paying taxes regularly on it. Later, when you are supporting yourself on earned income, it will be the same story, so you may as well get used to it now.

The Counterproposal

If the first offer is unacceptable, your next move may be a thoughtful, carefully worded counterproposal. It may help to explain gently but firmly exactly why certain parts of the offer were not possible for you to accept. Then show some creative thinking in your own offer. Demonstrate the fact that you know by now what this is all about.

If you are able to come up with a sophisticated proposal of your own at this juncture, and if you offer it in a perfectly agreeable and confident way, you may find that your husband and his attorney are suddenly taking a different tack with you. This wife, they suddenly realize, is not a witless creature after all. They are going to have to look at the whole situation in a different light. The next proposal is likely to be far more nearly acceptable.

Watch out, though, on the business of the IOU. Even if you are convinced that you *ought* to be awarded a certain amount, it may be more practical to offer an appealing discount to the other side if it is paid NOW. Let's assume that there is a shortage of ready cash, a very common situation these days! It's the old business of a bird in the hand being worth two in the bush. Things can change. Outside influences may come along to make it very difficult for you to collect later. The husband who can't come up with the cash may find a lender who can help him give you the entire amount he owes you right away. Better for him to owe the bank, very often, than to owe you. This can be true even where the interest he might offer on an IOU might be higher than that given by banks. It is a good idea to avoid having commingled moneys still hanging over you after the divorce. Get full control of your own money wherever you can.

Money and Children

Another word here about children. Try to keep the issue of their care and custody as separate from money matters as possible. I have seen fathers who would not really want to undertake the physical care of their children try anyway to use them, in a sort of attempt at emotional blackmail, during negotiations. They say, directly or indirectly, "I will take the children away from you if you don't accept thus and so and go away quietly." If this should happen to you, call for great firmness on the part of your attorney. Children should never be used as pawns in any situation. The person who ought to raise them is, very simply, the one who will give the time and energy necessary to do the job well. If you are this person, by all means be prepared to fight for them all the way.

Child-Support Payments

There is no finality to the issue of child custody. At any time, one or both parents may petition the court for a change. The goal here should be to give the best possible care to the child and to preserve decent relationships with both parents.

I think one reason there is so much trouble over child support payments is that fathers suspect this money is not being spent directly on the child; it is money no longer under the father's control. Also, if there is a jealous new wife, she may be trying to convince him that the money is being misused. Unless she is a very remarkable person, she will have some feeling that these sums should be spent on the new marriage; if she is a real neurotic, she will see money going out of her hands as a symbol of love that is not being given to her. This leaves Dad caught in a meat grinder, and we often see child-support payments being neglected as a result.

Now that so many people with children are divorcing and remarrying, I am convinced that we ought to set up more trusts to handle child-support funds. An objective third party can offer assurances to everyone involved that the funds are necessary and that they are being conscientiously handled. Child support should be set on a sliding scale so that children will benefit from future growth of the father's income. If inflation continues, this too should be provided for. A father who was convinced that his children were really benefiting from his contributions—and who had the opinions of the new wife firmly removed from this arena—might be far more willing to provide a fair deal.

Final Negotiations

In every situation, the final negotiations will be a little different. There can be some very sticky wickets here, and a great deal of work may have to be done on certain complex issues.

Some of the most difficult situations I have encountered have had to do with family-owned businesses. Here we are dealing with the couple who have built up a common interest in some enterprise over many years. Perhaps the wife has not actually been working in the office, but she has been a partner in any number of other ways. Now it is time to divide the assets fairly—but how to go about it? The courts do not like to see the woman remain after divorce as co-owner, except in rare instances where she is actually an employee on the grounds and where it is mutually agreeable for her to continue as such. There is wisdom in this point of view, for people who can't live together aren't usually able to work together satisfactorily either.

Jack and Sheila, for example, had worked very hard together, and after eighteen years the business was said to be worth millions. Because this was a privately owned company it was very difficult to determine its actual worth. They had accountants working on the problem for months, and finally they arrived at a figure. What next? They didn't want to sell the business to divide the assets, and no judge was going to demand the forced sale of such a thriving concern.

After a good deal of discussion about the possibility of borrowing so that Sheila could have her share in cash, the attorneys came up with the idea of having Jack issue an IOU to her instead for a rather large sum—over a million dollars. The total amount would be paid to Sheila, with interest, over the next ten years. Sounds great! But look what is going to happen from a tax point of view. This IOU is being amortized, meaning that both principal and interest are being paid off each month, and the entire amount will be taken care of at the end of the ten-year period. But in the meantime, the payments of the first few years are mostly interest, and interest payments are totally taxable to Sheila. She is going to end up paying most of her available income to the federal and state income tax bureaus and, even though she is a millionaire on paper, she may well find herself scratching around for grocery money.

What can she do? She does not want to jeopardize the growth of this company. She wants to be fair, and she knows that her husband will use some of his income to help support their children and see that they receive a good education. What she wants for herself is a square deal and a chance for a new life.

Here's how it was managed in the end: Sheila looked at all the facts and worked out a sensible long-term plan. She began by making a chart of her tax position throughout the ten years. She could see clearly then that she would not be receiving her own money back until the latter part of that period. She arranged to accept several hundred thousand dollars, which she invested mostly in real estate, along with the note for the remainder owed. Her investments were managed so as to offer her short-term tax advantages that helped her to a certain extent; but the crux of the matter was that she did not make the mistake of thinking of herself as a very rich woman, and she did not run out with the cash she received and begin spending it foolishly. Eventually Sheila became quite a successful businesswoman on her own. Best of all, this entire transaction was managed without hurting the business, which survived to help with her children's college costs.

The ideal situation, as mentioned before, is for the wife to receive a lump-sum settlement in cash. When this happens, she is not tied up with the tax situation we've just been looking at. Gillian's husband, for example, was an attorney who was able to borrow on his professional reputation to give her the entire amount agreed upon. He already had his next wife picked out, so he was in a mood to be very cooperative. Gillian got the family home and a sum to invest tax-free. Both partners were helped by this arrangement to cut the emotional ties that so often remain when there is continuing financial obligation. Gillian was in an especially good position now, disappointed though she was by the failure of her marriage, to turn that page over.

Doubtful Assets

There are certain kinds of assets that may better be left on the husband's side of the ledger now. During negotiation, you will want to avoid getting stuck with (1) something you would not be able to manage later to your own advantage, and (2) assets so doubtful that there is no way to determine whether or not they are of any value at all. Among the so-called assets that may be very hard for you to manage are not only properties your husband may have managed on some special, personal basis but also debts you might have trouble collecting yourself.

Sometimes there will be a stock of such doubtful value that you need tax advice on whether or not to accept it. You might want to keep it with the idea of selling it later at a capital loss, so as take a deduction on your income taxes. This sort of decision will require professional expertise. When you find yourself working out details such as this, you are probably nearing the end of the negotiating process. Don't hurry it just because you want to get it over with. On the other hand, don't become paranoid over the possibility that you may make a mistake. Mistakes are something everybody in this world occasionally makes, and you are going to be no exception.

Stalling

A curious thing sometimes happens at this stage of the negotiation. Even women who have done their homework with pencil and paper, and have done it well, may suddenly find themselves frozen, unable to make a single decision. The fact is that they are scared to death. All the trauma of the divorce seems to focus itself on the finality of an agreed-upon settlement. Remember that all of us are faced with decision-making, and there are many times in life when it isn't easy. All we can do is our very best, and then pick up the pieces and make up our minds to go on from there. Sure, you may have missed something. Yes, you may have regrets after all. But don't go on endlessly chewing it over and over. There comes a time when the best thing you can do is let it go.

Is Your Attorney Representing YOU?

What is your next move if you come to the conclusion during negotiating that your attorney is not doing the job as you would like to have it done? Must you simply bite the bullet and say nothing? Not at all. You have hired someone to represent you, and if you are not pleased with the situation, a meeting between you and this attorney should take place. For this, you should be tremendously well-prepared. You should be

isolate the trouble area and make a statement
.t. For example: *It seems to me that you are not
| into consideration the value of my husband's
partnership good will. I know it must be worth something, for he is named as a partner in this enterprise.
This item is not mentioned in your bargaining about
family assets, and I believe that it should be.* If you
have to bring up an issue like this, you may be getting
into a very delicate area.

Could it be that your husband is a well-known figure
in your town or city—and that your attorney may not
want to come into conflict here? An eager professional
on the way up can sometimes be persuaded by the position of the husband not to go out and shake that tree.
Or for some other reason there may be neglect, careless-
ness, real lack of commitment. If there really is no way
for you to proceed effectively with this particular attorney, a change must take place. You will have to have
your reasons clear, and you will have to pay your attorney's bill in full. You can receive copies of your papers
that are on file, but you will not receive the originals.
Why? Because if there are any challenges in the future
as to what took place, the law office will need those
documents.

Do you suspect collusion between the attorneys in
this case? Or some other form of malpractice? Be absolutely sure you have the facts if you intend to make a
complaint. If you have them, go ahead by all means.
The local bar association should hear about it, although
they may very well want to keep the matter quiet. Your
county district attorney or the state attorney general
would be the next ones to turn to if you really have a
case to present.

Before you go all-out for a change of attorneys, you
should have figured out the cost/benefit ratio of the
move. In other words, you should know the dollar value
of what you are fighting for in relation to the cost of

hiring another attorney at this point. The amount should be well into the tens of thousands, I think, to make this a useful change for you. A new attorney will have to go over the very same ground again, for preparation must be made in the most minute detail.

Your Next Attorney's Style

If you are going to change attorneys at this point, you probably expect to go to court for your final settlement. The situation is complicated and there is a certain amount of money and/or property involved. Be *very* careful, under such circumstances, to pick a new attorney who is skilled at prosecuting—who knows exactly how to handle himself or herself in court. Do some careful research on this score, and go to court yourself to watch for the kind of person you want to represent you in that particular situation. When you approach your next attorney, make it clear that you are ready and willing to go to court if necessary; he or she won't want to do all the preparation work and then have you back down.

Negotiating the Attorney's Fees

Toward the end of the negotiation process you may find that the attorney's fees become a major issue. There is often a good deal of jockeying back and forth between the two attorneys themselves on this issue. You should have your own estimate of the fee schedule well in hand, as suggested in an earlier chapter. Let me warn you here of a few situations of which you should be wary. Handle them with kid gloves.

If you have agreed to hire your attorney on a contingency basis—to offer a percentage of anything you may collect—you will have to take this into consideration when weighing your final moves. Usually this is done here has been some questionable aspect to the ...es involved or when there are features to this ...e that may not have come before the courts before. Your attorney may feel at some point that there is not going to be much percentage in continuing the negotiation process, and you must realize that this is one of the disadvantages of this system of payment from your point of view.

On the other hand, in a case involving very large fees, you may find that the opposing attorney wants to have your husband pay fees to your attorney in the form of alimony to you. This represents a tax deduction which is very nice for your husband, but it may leave you in a bad position. He may be paying, in effect, only about half of that fee because of the tax savings this arrangement gives him. But you know by now that *anything paid as alimony is taxable to you.* Who gets hurt in this arrangement? You do! It will probably be explained to you that the attorney will present a bill in such a way as to help you with taxes. It will state that at least 90 percent of the advice being charged for had to do with investments and income taxes; both these sorts of advice are also tax-deductible on your part. However, you should see this in writing and itemized properly before you take any chances whatever. If you accept extra checks with the instructions that you should then pay your attorney with them, you may find yourself owing a great deal of money to the government.

If that is the only basis on which your husband will undertake to pay your attorney's fees, what should you do? There is no hard-and-fast rule to follow here. If you have a good attorney, you will be guided very carefully in just such a situation. If this is the case, *be sure you are listening!* Too often either the attorney hadn't bothered to make this clear or the woman's mind was somewhere else at the time.

How Is He Getting Along?

What are some of the things your former spouse may be up to during the negotiating period? That, of course, depends at least partially on how long it takes. Some husbands decide to sulk and go on a deliberate "slowdown" of their work in an attempt to make the impression that they are suddenly poverty-stricken. If this happens, you can show that this is a ruse by producing careful records of past earnings for the court to consider.

Could it be, though, that your former spouse really is in a fragile condition? Could it be that some pressures at this time might jeopardize his health, so that future earnings will not be available to you and your children? In this case you may decide that this is not the time to press for financial advantage—even to discuss the final settlement. It might be better to make up your mind to a state of separation for a temporary period without negotiation until the coast is clear. In this connection I think particularly of those businessmen who must find willing lenders and investors in order to assure their own financial success. This is where you must tread softly indeed, and be very quiet about the divorce. If there are circumstances involved—you may be longing to tell them—not very flattering to him, you will do better to say nothing at all to the community at large. You can do without the pleasures of gossip if you really set your mind to it.

Taking Care of Yourself

Part of taking care of yourself during this period will consist of knowing deep down that it is going to take as long as it takes—no more, no less. You are involved in a transaction that will set the stage for all your future years, not only in terms of money but also in terms of emotional and physical health. You know by now what it means when we say that a sum of money is in escrow—it is being held out of the market temporarily while negotiations are under way. This, in fact, is what will be done to some of your family assets if they are sold during the divorce period. Now you are your own best asset: your talent, your strength, and your experience are the raw materials out of which you are going to construct the rest of your life. Think of yourself as if you were in escrow temporarily (a guarded asset, it is sometimes called) and be sure to guard yourself accordingly. Sometimes it takes more than months— it may actually take a year or two—for a man to recognize the reality of the law. It may take a woman that long to understand that she can't sue for a broken heart. She can only sue for assets due to her.

After being intimately involved with hundreds of women who have gone through the process of divorce, I have come to realize that there simply must be a period of grief. A process of adjustment must be allowed to take place. So be it. *Let the logic of events take place* is a piece of advice my own father passed on to me, and I often think of it when working with women in the divorce situation. I want my clients to take very good care of themselves right now. I like to see them exercise regularly and avoid overeating, oversmoking, overdrinking, and the foolish use of drugs. But don't decide that you are going to lose thirty pounds right now, *and* give up smoking, *and* take courses in nineteen different subjects, *and* take on a new job. This is no time to run out and conquer the world all at once. Make up your mind that you are going to tackle any bad habits you may have one at a time, on a definite schedule. Of course *you can do anything* when you have got your act together. For now, though, slow down a little and smell a few roses.

Can It Be Over?

Some day it will be. The messenger or the mailman will be delivering the final proposal, the one you have decided to accept. I have seen women actually unable to open this envelope. It has been such a long time, and it has been for some of them such a hard struggle. This mood can very easily turn into something quite unreasonable: "No, I won't sign! Why are they being pushy? I'll just make them wait until I am ready!"

Well, if you and your attorney are convinced that this is the proposal you ought to sign, and if you have read it over very carefully, making certain that it is all exactly as agreed upon, pick up that pen and get going! Don't waste a moment now on if onlys. This is the reality you have been waiting for—the fairest solution you could possibly manage under the circumstances. It isn't going to be perfect: nothing in life is perfect. The important thing is that you are in motion again; tomorrow is going to be a really new day.

Chapter 8

ON YOUR OWN: FINANCIAL PLANNING FOR YOUR FUTURE

IT'S ALL OVER at last. After months of uncertainty about the outcome, you know now exactly what to expect. You may or may not have the family home; you may or may not have the assets you hoped to see turning up on your side of the settlement; *but it is settled.* There will be no more wakeful nights, wondering.

Many of you will still be hurting. You will want to lash out at the unfairness of it all. You are convinced that you should have had more than this. Don't look back! Just say to yourself "I did the best I could," and let it go. It's time for you to turn away from all this and go find some sunlight to put into your life.

Shelter for a Woman

As noted before, a woman's environment—her home base—is deeply important to her. It is a part of her as it is seldom part of the man's psyche. And in practical ways too, it is the shelter she offers to her children, to her friends for meeting and entertaining, to her community as an expression of herself. The first thing to do when you have gotten your final settlement is to look around at your place of residence and do what you can very cheaply, very simply, to make it as attractive and inviting as possible.

For those of you who will seek new shelter—keep this in mind. Living nicely has nothing to do with the number of rooms, the square footage, the expense of the place. It has to do with how you take control of that area so that it is charming and clean and thoroughly pleasant to be in. I remember that during the war, when I was moving from place to place to be with my husband, I always brought with me just a few personal things that helped me dress up the crummiest of rented rooms: a pair of silver candlesticks, an heirloom quilt, two crystal goblets. A trip to the neighborhood market would get me a couple of sweet potatoes or yams. I'd stick some toothpicks around them to support them in a water glass, and within a week we had our green vines started. Wherever we were, that space became a little part of heaven. Even if you are alone now—most especially, if you are alone—you should do this for yourself. Set the table for yourself with your very best china. Sit down to a meal, however simple, that you have prepared with great care. Light the candles! Let yourself be your own honored guest.

Your entertaining is going to be simpler now, less expensive in all probability. Never mind. A spaghetti dinner for your teenage children's friends and a few well-chosen neighbors can be a lot more fun than those sit-down dinners for twelve that used to cost so much time and money. You get to choose the guest list completely now. Whether you're living temporarily or permanently in the family home; whether you're already on the move to a smaller place; always think of your home with pride, and always think of it in terms of sharing its pleasures with others.

Are You Moving?

"How can you possibly move away from family and friends?" people once asked me at a transition point in my own life. My reply was that I would rent a truck, get a strong youngster to help me load up, and drive away—that's how I would do it. "Oh, but Mary," they said. "What if you don't like it in the new place? What if you are lonely and it just doesn't work out?" Well then, you just rent another truck and load up again and come back. The point is not to be afraid to try something new. Don't be one of those people who ends up sitting in a rocking chair sighing about "Oh, if I had only . . . ."

If you are moving, eliminate as many possessions as you possibly can. Put the rest in storage. Prepare yourself for some new experiences, new horizons. Don't rush in and buy the first thing that appeals to you, at a price you think you can afford, in a new neighborhood. Consider renting for a while instead. Test more than one situation, if need be. You must be very careful about choosing your permanent location. "But I have to buy," some clients say, "because I postponed my payment of taxes on the sale of our family home. I have to hurry now, or I'll be in financial trouble." No, you won't. You have eighteen months before you lose that tax privilege, and you can do a lot of experimenting in that length of time—particularly now that you're not in a stew over the final settlement. Constant moving about, of course, would be just plain dumb. But look at your options—make some lists for yourself—and try out some of the possible ways of life that might work for you in, say, the next five years. If you have children, don't forget to include a forecast of their needs in your plans; they will grow up faster than you think. They will want to move out or share space with young people their own age while working or going to college. Maybe they have already reached that blessed state, in which case you are *really* ready to take off!

How to Find Rentals

Suppose you want to try a new neighborhood. You have decided to put the old memories aside and enjoy them later—meantime, you are going to try for some new ones! Where do you begin? Of course, you can always read the newspapers and go to real estate agents. But many of the best rentals are never listed. I would start with the most elegant part of town, and be so bold as to ring doorbells saying that I was looking for a place to rent and asking people whether they knew of anything that might be available. I would have some cards printed, giving my name and either a post-office box number or a telephone number where I could be reached. I would make myself known in the neighborhood, and I would visit the local churches, the temples, the social organizations. The priest, the minister, and the rabbi often know more about what is going on in town than the people down at the newspaper. Many of the larger, older homes are now being broken up into apartments. Servants' quarters and cottages on the grounds are being rented to help pay for rising costs and taxes. You might very well be one who finds a real gem of a living situation for yourself this way.

You will find that children and pets, of course, are not wanted in some places that might be very desirable. This may be the time for you to make some tough decisions! You can't send your kids off anywhere COD, but you must be willing to look at a pet as something you could do without at this time. Be honest with landlords about the existence of children and/or pets in your life. It doesn't work to spring these into the situation as "little surprises."

Sharing Shelter—a Possible Answer

The more people you talk to, the more people you inform about your search for shelter, the wider your sphere of influence will be. Along the way, consider the possibility of sharing. Two women, especially those with children, may find it greatly to their advantage to share the rent of a larger place than either could afford alone. A larger yard, a two-car garage—but above all, the companionship and mutual help with child care and other tasks can be a tremendous plus to the divorced woman.

Will there be a great adjustment to make? Of course there will. One can't move from one's own little box to a sharing situation without a good deal of give-and-take. You do what you have to do. Just be sure you *write down* all your guidelines and have them thoroughly understood before moving in together. Then, if both of you really want it to work, you've got a very good chance of success.

The Condominium

Do not rush out and buy a condominium if you can rent one first in the complex that interests you. Of course, the interest and property taxes you will pay on purchase will be tax-deductible items and will thus serve to reduce your income taxes. On the other hand, there is a cost of buying, of setting up the mortgage at one end and at the other, there is the cost of selling. You might purchase a condo because you want control over your shelter costs and because the mortgage payments don't increase over the years of the contract. Remember, if this is the case, that other costs probably *will* go up: maintenance, property tax, insurance.

The most important thing to understand in purchasing a condominium is that you are going to be a part of a community. This community actually makes the laws, the policies of operation, and even determines the cost of maintaining your home and grounds. The community can be run very efficiently or quite poorly, depending on the quality of the people on the governing board. Some of us *must* own, if at all possible, simply for our peace of mind. If you are one of these, a condominium in an area you have thoroughly explored and evaluated may be just the ticket for you. Just don't hurry into anything, because this is going to be your home, as surely as if you were buying a house—and you are not going to have sole control of its management.

What about Inflation?

You may have a sum of cash in your hands now (from your settlement or from the sale of the family home) and for some of you, this will be a heady new experience. On all sides you will hear that real estate is one of the best possible hedges against inflation. From real estate agents you may hear that it is the one sure thing. You may even be urged to buy something you cannot realistically afford—or don't even particularly like, deep down—just because it sounds as if this were a safe way to protect the value of your money. It ain't necessarily so!

Not all real estate is going to grow in value. The cost of buying too hastily can turn that expected increase into zero, especially with too many moves and too many attached costs.

Changing Styles

One of the smartest women I know determined that she couldn't continue to live in *the* neighborhood after her divorce, and then she looked around and decided that her entire county was far too expensive for her and her children. She could remember a small town she had once visited and loved. She took the time to go back there and explore the possibilities. To her great joy, she found that she could buy a nice little house in this town, the right size for her family and not too large when the children should leave for college. She found that this town had educational opportunities for her own re-entry into the working world. The job possibilities were going to be within commuting distance— and so she moved boldly into that situation, to her great financial and emotional advantage. We all know that there are certain areas where the prices of homes have become inflated beyond reason. Do we really *have* to live there? Of course we don't. There are other places, perhaps not too far away, where there are still small houses in very nice neighborhoods, affordable to the person on a budget.

The Mobile Home

Don't say "No! I could never!" to the idea of a mobile-home park as a possibility for you. You could, too, because you can do anything you want to do at this point. The mobile home is one way for a woman of limited means to live quite nicely. There are going to be problems, as there are whenever people live in close contact with one another. But there are going to be some problems wherever you go. You might find a mobile-home park that was quite attractive with very agreeable neighbors. A mobile home tends to sell for $15,000 to $75,000, and many of them are comfortable to the point of being positively luxurious. It's to your advantage that in most parks you will find units to rent temporarily while you make up your mind as to whether or not you want to stay on. Think about it—and do some investigation, if this seems like a reasonable possibility for you.

Lifetime Care

If you are getting on in years, the very phrase *lifetime care* may sound charming at the time of a painful divorce. You want someone to *care for* you and you don't stop to think whether you mean nursing care or the other kind. Well, get your thoughts in order before you try to purchase something along these lines that you may very well not need. In other words, don't put your money down on a lifetime-care-community situation until you are very sure exactly what you are buying and why you are buying it.

Madge came down with a bad case of flu just after her divorce and immediately hit the panic button. She was unused to being alone, and she had never felt so helpless. What would happen to her, she wondered, if she should become seriously ill? Several elderly widows she knew had opted for apartments in a lifetime-care community where their medical and nursing care, as needed, was guaranteed in return for a hefty purchase price and a monthly fee. Madge was only sixty-two and was basically strong—a fact she had forgotten for the moment—but she hurried out to buy into the long-term-care situation as soon as she felt well enough to take a walk. Perhaps it was the only way she could find peace of mind, and if so, then I guess it was something she simply had to do. I would have preferred to see her make a pact with several friends and/or neighbors for the time being, stating that they would be available to check on each other's needs when temporary illness struck and to run simple errands for one another. Then I would have liked to see her get up her nerve to try for a more creative, more independent style of living, at least until she was a good deal older than sixty-two.

We all need *care,* of course, and if the kind you

need is the kind you can buy, go ahead and buy it. Investigate the community of your choice very thoroughly, though. Talk to people who have been living there for some time. Are they satisfied? Some of these institutions have had financial problems, especially with an inflationary economic situation, and have not been able to supply all of the services that had been promised. Look at the grounds and the buildings—are they well kept? Are the medical and nursing services really of fine quality? How would you feel about living here when you were *not* ill? What would your neighbors be like? What are the transportation possibilities? Would you become isolated? Are there books, lectures, musical evenings, crafts, and group activities available? Be realistic about the needs of your mind and emotions as well as of your body when making the decision to buy lifetime care. Then go for it, if that is what you really want.

Warning: Just because a lifetime-care facility is sponsored by a religious group or a church doesn't necessarily mean that it is sound from a financial point of view. Your research of the financial aspects here should be done in depth. The Better Business Bureau can help you, and you may want to send off a letter as well to your state attorney general's office or your state department of corporations. Ask, and you shall find out.

My advice on shelter has to do basically with your peace of mind. Don't buy too quickly or move too often. Rent where possible, and be prepared to spend up to 50 percent of your monthly income at this particular point in your life to rent a place that gives you feelings of security and self-esteem. Later on your anxiety will be diminished. You need to do the best you possibly can for yourself now, to establish a nest you can feel safe in, and to share it with happiness and pride. Be good to yourself, and choose well!

Money Management

Now you have your living situation and it is time for you to make some solid financial plans for your future. Let us assume that you have received some cash and/or some property in your divorce settlement. You also have some income from your own earnings and/ or temporary alimony. You may be tempted to think you are rather well off, after all: there is the sight of actual cash, clearly belonging to you. How easy it is going to be right now for you to begin spending money above your budget! We can all rationalize those extra costs. A little of that cash from the settlement here and a little there (on something important to me, of course) can't matter very much, can it? You bet it can! Hold on! Don't dip into that particular pot *at all.*

The settlement you have received, whether invested in your home, in stocks, or in cash should now be considered your *old age pension.* Come hell, high water, or another man, don't compromise that money. Rarely can the woman entering the work force at midlife be fortunate enough to secure a viable retirement plan. I wish she could, but it has been my experience that she will have nothing to fall back on after that last paycheck comes in. The assets from her divorce settlement, carefully invested, may be all she has to support her during those crucial years between sixty and eighty—or even beyond. I don't want you to be old, alone and poor, *ever.* Lock up your assets for now, in a safe, short-term, high-yield money market investment, while you make plans. You are going to need time to investigate a longer-term commitment of this money. If some of it is going into stocks, you'll need a slow, steady education in that field. If it is in real estate, you are going to have a lot of homework to do. In the meantime, don't let cash sit in an ordinary checking or savings account: put it to work for you while you think things over and learn what you need to learn.

The figures on this chart can help you to be your own financial planner. Determine a goal for yourself (say, a certain amount of money by the age of sixty) and invest the right amount to achieve that at one of the higher percentages listed below. Make up your mind *nothing* will cause you to abandon this plan or begin nibbling away at that capital. Here's how it works:

For $10,000 invested with earnings compounded annually:

	5 yrs.	*10 yrs.*	*20 yrs.*
8%	$14,690	$21,590	$46,600
10%	16,100	26,000	67,275
12%	17,620	31,000	96,463

Lump sum required to reach $100,000:

	5 yrs.	*10 yrs.*	*20 yrs.*
8%	$68,000	46,300	21,450
10%	62,000	38,554	14,864
12%	56,743	32,197	10,367

How long will $100,000 last, invested at 8%?

Income per month	*Number of years*
$ 666	just interest, indefinitely
730	30
835	20
955	15
1210	10

How about Inflation?

It's wise to be aware of the inflation problem, but you should not be scared out of your skin about it. When we hear that the inflation rate is 8 to 9 percent based on cost-of-living averages, this doesn't always mean that you will experience the same increase in buying ordinary necessities. The inflation index is based largely on the borrowing of money to buy shelter or to purchase a car. The place where we all experience those price increases is at the market, buying food. We can also assume that medical care will continue to rise—and yet, not all individuals over sixty are in need of medicine. Old age is not a disease.

I cannot give you an answer on how to stay ahead of inflation. As you progress in knowledge about investments, I hope you will feel able to put *some* of your money into the riskier situations that offer higher rates of earning if all goes well; but even after you become something of an expert, you shouldn't put it all, or even a very large percentage of it, there. Instead, the financially inexperienced woman should try to increase her income by reducing her expenditures. She should reexamine her values, simplify her life-style, and try to receive the highest earning on her savings that she can possibly manage *with safety.* The money market funds are a good place to begin on this project. The yield will be far greater than on most passbook accounts, there is no charge for investment on many of these funds, and you will find that many of them also offer a kind of flexibility that makes them particularly convenient: you can withdraw your funds very easily at any time, writing checks on your money market account for $500 or more. There are no penalties for withdrawals, as there are apt to be on other high-earning savings plans. Investigate, either by reading *The Wall Street Journal,* or *The Weisenberger Market Fund Reports* (found in the library) unless you already have an account with a brokerage house, which will handle this investment for you if you wish.

Managing versus Making Money

As you move along, after the first year or so you may become more knowledgeable and thus more confident about taking some risks. But understand that there is a difference between managing money and making it. Making money always involves some element of risk. Before you do that, you must have learned much and you must have control of your immediate situation by means of careful planning for your running expenses and cautious placement of capital funds in safe situations.

It is time for you to take another look at your Financial Notebook now. Study the records of your recent expenditures and make any adjustments that may be needed for your budget. If you have "borrowed" out of dire necessity from your savings, this is the time for you to make every possible effort to pay that money back to yourself. Try to keep your finances as simple as possible at this time. You have enough to contend with, getting yourself into motion—learning new employment skills, going back to school, or whatever you have decided in terms of your own future.

Are you going to need an accountant from now on? Many a woman leaves the attorney's office at the close of her case with the advice that an accountant will be an absolute necessity. Perhaps one has been invaluable during the negotiation period. Still, do some research before deciding this question. Most lawyers assume that a female client has never dealt with the question of income taxes and wouldn't know where to begin; therefore the accountant enters the picture more or less automatically. But, unless you are involved with the sale of the family home, a business, or some stock, you may not need the professional service now. Even if you must sell something, how about getting the facts together and then making an appointment with the best tax accountant in town with some specific questions in mind? The time for counsel is before the act, not after; but you may be able to get what you need in a thirty-minute appointment and save yourself a wad of money if you are well organized.

What about filing your income taxes? Does the thought of doing it on your own cause total dismay? Why don't you open the forms that are mailed to you in January and just see how far you can go with them? We have already talked about filing the estimated tax statement and paying quarterly. It may be that you will be able to fill in those blanks as well as anyone else. Then if you wish, or if you have questions, you can go to the local Internal Revenue Service office and ask them to check over what you have done. If the very thought of taxes leaves you weak, don't be ashamed to ask for the help you need. Nevertheless, I think most of you really can handle it quite well.

Whose Responsibility?

Mabel had never made a financial decision in her life. Now she was given a settlement consisting of a very large amount of stock in one of the most prestigious companies in the world. The shares had been bought so long ago that their value was now almost entirely profit. One person told her that the simplest thing for her to do was just sell a few shares whenever she needed funds and let it go at that. Someone else told her that it was dangerous to have all her eggs in one basket, even when the company was The Best. Mabel didn't know what to do. Feeling fragile, she tiptoed in to see an investment counselor. The office had thick rugs and a receptionist with a British accent. Immediately, Mabel felt more secure.

She walked into the inner sanctum and a paternal gentleman assured her that he would take care of her investment. *There would be nothing for her ever to worry about!* He asked her how much money she would need per month to live on. She answered as best she could; then she was informed that a special account would be set up at a convenient bank and would be at her disposal. The amount she requested would be placed in that account each and every month. There would be a slight fee for the investment management and for the bank account. That was all. *How marvelous,* thought Mabel.

A few years later, Mabel attended one of my lectures and her eyes began to open. She began asking some questions of her investment counselor and found him curiously reluctant to reply, strangely evasive in his manner toward her. Finally, after months of worry, being told "You don't need to know" or "Don't bother," she got the facts—and they were not pretty.

The gentleman in question had sold a large portion of the Great Stock and had bought three items. One of the purchases had been bought for thirty dollars a share and was now worth three dollars. One was purchased for "increased income" though the dividend it paid was little better than the amount from a 5 percent passbook account. The third had been devalued about 50 percent since its purchase, and again the dividend was meager. Meantime, the money coming from the sale was taxable, so the following year another portion of her stock had to be sold to obtain money for the tax bill. Poor judgment in each and every move! If diversification was needed, it should have been done carefully to avoid triggering of excessive tax situations. The quality of repurchases was so poor as to form an issue that could have been brought before the Securities and Exchange Commission. At no time had this adviser tried to educate the client about her responsibility or her choices. He never suggested that she should change a few of her investments to increase her monthly income, saving the remaining shares as a hedge against inflation and a benefit for her old age. He went along without considering her welfare in the least, doing whatever occurred to him at the time. He must have known that all her funds would be used up some day, but perhaps he thought that she would be dead by then!

This should be a lesson to every woman who is thinking of turning over her assets to an investment adviser. Some of these individuals will do an excellent job for you. Others will not. But the responsibility for your money is still yours, no one else's. Mabel's situation would have been much less catastrophic if she had had the nerve to challenge her adviser long before she finally did—by then it was very nearly too late. Make up your mind that you are going to have a plan of your own, and work with that. Use your professionals to help you educate yourself. Supervise their every move, and ask to see every document. Don't let transactions happen without your approval, and don't be embarrassed to keep asking questions about those transactions until you understand them. A person who really knows his stuff is able to explain it—and not in technical language, either, but in terms you can understand. If he can't explain it to you, chances are he doesn't really know what he is talking about—or doesn't want you to know.

Con Artists

This brings us to the subject of con artists. Unfortunately, these creatures do exist, and you will do well to watch out for them. Remember that the notice of your divorce has been published in the local newspaper. There are people who read these notices either for the purpose of selling you something or arranging to cheat you in ways that are sometimes quite elaborate.

Who are these people? Where would you be apt to meet them? I hate to say it, but you may even meet them in church. I know of one slick character who made it onto the vestry of his church, served two terms, and ran through the fortunes of several local women before being discovered. Don't become paranoid on this score; just be aware that your changed situation will be known by a great many people very quickly, and that all of them won't have your own best interests at heart. The best rule to follow is: Make no moves whatever at this time unless you are very sure about the person you are dealing with and very certain about the product that is being sold. Remember, *there is no such thing as a financial transaction without a fee.*

You may be invited to a great many free forums and lectures about investments, tax shelters, and estate planning at this time. I am not saying that you should avoid anything like this, for you may become educated about finances as a result. Just don't kid yourself that the purpose of these gatherings is to educate you. Their purpose is to obtain clients for the company that is presenting the forum. Don't you forget it! Look for the hidden motive whenever you are offered something by way of a deal that is going to make you a lot more money than you could expect from the usual investment—and look for it whenever you are offered something "for free."

Here is an example. This one is called the Ponzi Plan (or Game, or Ruse). An innocent is approached with an idea for an investment that sounds terrific. It may be in stock, gold, land, fish—anything—but the rewards of this investment are going to be greater than anything you've ever heard of before, our victim is told. "You may join the select group of investors!" she hears. "This is only for the chosen few." On a down payment of, say, $5,000 you are going to get a large dividend almost immediately. And the funny thing is, you do.

It is quite a large check, many times more than you are receiving on other accounts, Treasury Bills, or whatever you might have invested in until now. So what would any smart person do? When they call to ask you whether you received the check and ask you to put in a little more (say, $20,000) of course you can't wait to do just that. In a couple of months another very large check comes in, proving that you have made a brilliant investment (or does it?). By now you have told all your friends about the deal, and some of them have invested too. What a lucky break for everybody involved! The trouble is that the next check should be coming along in about six months, and it doesn't. You wait, thinking it must have been delayed in the mail. Nothing happens. You were counting on that check! You call the office to inquire—and there isn't any office. The nice man who always used to answer the phone has vanished and the number has been disconnected.

You've been had. The "dividends" you received were not from any investment. The money received by the "investors" was never invested. Your own money or your friends' money was being dribbled back at you to keep you quiet until the con artists felt it was time to disappear. Then they took off—and chances are very good that you will never see any of that money again. What did you do wrong? You were dumb. You didn't investigate the project. You didn't take time to phone the Better Business Bureau or the attorney general's office in the state in which you live to find out with whom you were dealing. You responded to someone's request for *hurry* on a deal. You were flattered to think that you had been chosen as a special investor—and you were greedy. I hope nothing like this will happen to you, but if it does, pick up the pieces and move on. You've learned a hard lesson at a great price. Tears won't help. Just make up your mind you are never going to do such a silly thing again.

Family Matters

A very delicate situation that must be mentioned next is family. You have your settlement now and everyone is suddenly aware that this involves *money*. The whole family, from Uncle George down to Baby Sue, is going to want to help you manage that money, and they are all going to give you plenty of advice. This is called "the pooling of ignorance." How should you respond? Bring out the useful sentence "That is very interesting" once more. Be very gracious and say nothing more than that. Then go ahead and do what *you* think is best for yourself after you have become educated. They won't be the ones who will educate you, especially if they are children or financially inexperienced young adults. This is a group of citizens—however charming and delightful they may be—with no sense of reality whatever about large sums of money.

A mother is a mother is a mother, always and forever, I know. But you have to be more than this now. You have to be your own financial manager too. What does a mother say when the young son comes around and asks for a loan to buy a car or to make a down payment for a vine-covered cottage for himself and his bride? He promises to pay her a better rate of interest than she could get from a savings account, pointing out that everyone will be helped this way—no one will be hurt.

I would tell that young man "I am sorry, but I cannot give you a loan. My money is all invested in long-term situations." Or, if circumstances permitted, I would say "I cannot give you a loan but I will be glad to make you a gift of the amount you need." It never works to mix family matters with business deals. Mother lends the money; the payments come in on time for a few months and then they stop coming. Feelings are strained on all sides. Mother is hurting and yet she does not want to press for what is owed her; son feels guilty and does not want to face her, but he has her on the bottom of the list of people he now owes just because she is his mother.

It would be much better for this mother to set aside a certain proportion of her settlement money—10 percent or 15 percent—if she can manage it, and make up her mind that this will be spent over a period of time on gifts to her children for their education, travel, help with major purchases, and so forth. Label this money *gifts* and use it freely in a way that is really enjoyable. If the amount is very small, remember that the number-one thing you owe your children is a happy, independent mother. If the kids can't find enough money to make that down payment on the home, maybe it wasn't time for them to have it yet. You don't do them a favor by acting as their banker and then expecting them to be grateful to you. You do better by setting them a good example in the management of your own life and by offering them your love, your interest and concern, your advice when asked for—and a listening ear. Money is the *least* of what they need from you.

Being Beautiful

A great many of you are going to be feeling battered, tired, and somewhat less than attractive at this point in your life. It's part of the self-esteem problem that goes along with divorce. I've said before that you should do nice things for yourself, and treat yourself at meals like an honored guest. Now, as we prepare for re-entry into the larger world, look in a very cool and practical way at your own appearance. What can be done to improve it? Your spirits will expand when the outside of the package is put in order; you will also find that you are much more employable when you look your best. Even if it goes against the grain for you to pamper yourself or take trouble over your appearance at this point, do it as *an investment in yourself.*

What you need could be as simple as a visit to the beauty salon and a dye job, or it could be as elaborate as a nose job or a face lift. Whatever it is, if you can possibly afford it—go get it. Buy yourself a couple of really smashing new outfits now, and take time to perfect your grooming habits. If you are not already involved in learning a new job skill or training for a profession, plan to do some redecorating inside your head as well as outside. Go to school and begin studying hard toward a degree of some sort. The discipline involved will pay off, and association with younger people will help you with all your other re-entry problems. You're not going to vegetate for a minute now! Pretty soon, you yourself are going to be looking and feeling much younger too.

Chapter 9

BACK IN THE WORLD AGAIN

YOU'RE ON YOUR WAY NOW, learning how to be a self-supporting person in the larger world. Whether or not you've ever "worked" before, begin by throwing away all the old ideas you may have had about yourself in relation to the labor market. This may very well be the first time in your life that you have ever been free to do anything, be anything you want. There are exciting options and choices ahead of you. Make up your mind to explore them all. Get out that pencil and paper again and let's do some "brainstorming."

Just a Housewife

All of us are sick and tired by now of hearing that weary, apologetic phrase "just a housewife." Gradually in the past few years it has been dawning on our consciousness that this is the wrong way of putting it. If you have been running a household all these years, you know perfectly well that you are an experienced person, accustomed to taking serious responsibilities. You have learned to deal with all kinds of harrowing situations. You have wrestled with various sorts of machinery, and you have developed social skills with people of all ages and all kinds. You have been, in your own way, a top-level executive. If your children are grown, you are free to go anywhere, to work at any hour of day or night that you choose. If they are still small, you will want to design your new program around their needs, but you must go ahead and design it.

While you are at it, don't underestimate the market value of *any* volunteer experience you may have had. I give a great deal of credit for my success to the time I spent actively working for the League of Women Voters, while raising my child. Those were the years when I needed the balance of motherhood and continuing education—and the League taught me skills that have been tremendously useful in the professional world. Have you raised money for a health organization, or done political work, or organized a new enterprise in your community? Make a list of *all* your achievements and *all* your talents, inside the home and outside. This will be the beginning of a resume that will show just what you have to offer. When you go into the job market, you will be ready to sell yourself—because that is what it's all about.

Goodbye to Labels

Perhaps you worked for a while long ago as a schoolteacher or as a secretary. Is that what you really want to do now? Maybe it is. But if you know how to type, don't admit it at the moment; don't get trapped into believing that that's all you can do. The same goes for teaching. If you have been a teacher, you are an educated woman and you have all the building blocks for a new career. The only thing to bring forward from the past is the *total spectrum* of your life and your activities. Don't lock yourself into thinking "I am a secretary" or "I am a schoolteacher" unless that is the only thing you really want to do. Many employers are looking for mature women who have the energy, ambition, and tenacity to work well in some very demanding new kinds of situations.

Flo, a forty-five-year-old woman, telephoned me to tell me of her excitement in finding a job that was absolutely right for her. It seems that there was a brand-new company staffed mainly by bright young people who needed an "office manager." She went in for an interview and quickly came to the conclusion that what they really needed was a *mother*—a mature woman who was not flighty, who had good judgment and poise, who could help to hold that small band together. Flo had coped with a family, handling crisis after crisis without blowing her top, and she was accustomed to having people depend on her. She moved into the job easily and became a one-woman support system for the entire company. I'm sure there are many situations like this waiting for the talents of women who have no previous experience in the world of industry. Flo created her own job, in a sense, and there was no proper title or label for it.

Career Counseling

The job market is a fluid thing today. Only a few years back, we expected people to stay in the same line of work all their lives and perhaps to have their children follow on with that same occupation after them. Nowadays it is not unusual for a woman *or* a man to change occupations several times during a lifetime. Partly for this reason, there are now literally hundreds of organizations designed to help individuals with their employment problems; many of these address themselves specifically to the needs of women who are entering (or re-entering) the labor market. Look in your local newspaper for their announcements. Go to your state employment agency and find out what forums they offer. Local, state, and federal government agencies offer many programs in aid of the woman seeking "reentry." Local colleges often offer counseling about job opportunities. And there are individual experts who can be hired, if you can afford their fees and believe they may be particularly useful to you, to help you diagnose your talents, organize your resumes, get your long-term ambitions into better perspective. Anyone can read the want ads in the daily newspaper. I hope you will do more than this! Think creatively about your future career. Be innovative, be bold—and go out and get yourself all the help you may need. Only when you have identified your goals in your own mind is it time to roll up your sleeves and go on to work.

The Interview

Don't set up job interviews at all unless you can go in with a positive attitude, looking forward to meeting someone new and to listening with great interest to information about exactly what this company consists of and what it is planning to do. Whether or not the job is offered to you, make sure the person across the desk is aware that you are a woman of some real talent. This job, even though you did not get it, might be the springboard to something else. The personnel manager at this firm may be the one to suggest another opportunity that will work for you.

Now, what do *you* want from this job? Your own ideas on this, as well as the salary you expect, should be put forward to any future employer. I would hope that you might be willing to accept some minor position for a limited time, with the agreement of the boss that there would be opportunities for advancement. Some firms have an advancement ladder for you to consider, showing you how to prepare yourself for the higher ranks and better salaries by taking special classes or otherwise improving your skills. The interview should be a step in self-education, and at the same time you should be prepared to educate the potential employer as to your own goals. If you show real enthusiasm and ambition, you will have a much better chance at getting this job or having another possible opening suggested to you.

I'm Too Old

Too old for what? Lately I've begun to hear thirty-year-olds complaining about the traumatic effect of that particular birthday! At the same time, the federal agencies are beginning to hire senior citizens in all sorts of interesting capacities: for example, many are being trained to do paralegal work to help their fellow seniors. Old isn't a number, it's a state of mind. If you are forty or fifty or sixty years old and age is a big thing with you, it is bound to be a major consideration for the potential employer. Otherwise, he might not think twice about it. Suppose he or she brings up the problem of an insurance or pension plan for which you don't qualify because of your age? Don't let that throw you. By now you know something about managing money on your own; you can reply in a poised manner that, with sufficient salary for your work, you will be enabled to set up your own retirement and insurance plans; or you can ask the employer to cooperate by inventing a way around this obstacle. Make up your mind that your age is something you are going to be proud of, because it is evidence of the wealth of experience you have had.

The Nontraditional Job

I am aiming to free you from old, inflexible patterns of thought as you move into this exciting time of your life. You mustn't undervalue yourself and at the same time you mustn't have any truck with what I can only call false pride. Suppose, for example, that you have enough money from your settlement—and you are not going to touch that, remember? It is invested well, so you do not have to earn a great deal. You are free to get a part-time job, one that is personally rewarding to you. If this is the case, how about exploring the real needs of people around you? Don't automatically downgrade jobs like housekeeping, babysitting, chauffeuring, caring for the frail, the handicapped, the ill. These are services desperately needed by many families. You can be your own boss in these situations, and you can probably find work to suit you very near your own home. Wages may be generous, and you will have the profound satisfaction, especially if you have been missing your own grown children, of feeling deeply needed and appreciated. Helping an exhausted young mother in this way can actually create two happy mothers once again.

And there are plenty of other possibilities you may not have considered. What about the jobs men have always taken in the past? The ones using various kinds of power equipment? The power in this situation comes not from male muscle but from the fact that the man has learned which lever to pull. Couldn't you learn that, too? The average hourly wage for such work is probably more than twice what you could get by typing. That's one reason why I said not to mention it if you can type.

Maybe you'd like to work outside. Have you always been happy at the thought of gardening? I have known enterprising women who have worked as gardeners in their own communities—hauling manure and all the rest of it—while studying landscape design. One is now in business for herself as a landscaper, hiring others to do the dirty work, but she still, in her late 70s, putters around supervising and rearranging things for her clients' pleasure. She wears the smile of a happy and fulfilled woman, and she is healthy as a horse. You can travel now, if your children are pretty much on their own. Would you like to be a traveling saleswoman? A truckdriver? A lecturer on a cruise ship? Think big! What do you know already that might be useful in preparing yourself for such a job? As to the rest of it—well, are you or are you not trainable? I bet you are. Selling, especially, can be financially very rewarding. If you can find a product that you can believe in, and go on the road with that even though it is very hard work you can do very well indeed for your bank account. In the right selling situation, the sky's the limit, in fact.

What about My Spousal Support?

When I am advising a client about getting to work and making money, she will sometimes say "Oh, but Mary, I couldn't do that now, because my alimony would be taken away from me if it could be shown that I don't need it, that I am making money on my own." My answer to this is, first of all, "Show me the money you are making yourself, before you panic!" and then "Please do *not* forget your long-term goal!"

Spousal support or alimony is being paid to you for one reason—to help you establish yourself as an independent person. It is *not* a payoff for the injury you have received or the unhappiness you have suffered. It is an effort on the part of the court to push you forward in the world. If you are so fortunate and so hard-working that you suddenly begin to make a good deal of money, so much the better. I would say "Kindly stop my spousal support—I can take care of myself!" What a day that would be! Why lock yourself into the role of a dependent any longer than you really have to? Get on with your life—and don't look back.

Working at Home

If you have small children, the story is going to be a little different for you, of course. You certainly are going to need alimony during those years when your place is primarily with them. In that so-called spare time of yours, however, you can be taking courses to improve your job position against the day when you will be able to work full time. The woman who is in dire need of income during this period might consider babysitting other children while she is caring for her own, or developing a co-op with other mothers in the neighborhood who must also work. To this woman I say "Find some way to get yourself out of the house, by all means!" You have to go out and find the world—it won't come to you. Don't let yourself vegetate.

There are many support groups and cooperative groups available for this young mother, if she will look for them. Single Parents is one that has a good reputation. Volunteer groups, the American Association of University Women, the League of Women Voters, and other groups can also be very helpful in enlarging horizons. The trivial, everyday problems and catastrophes that can drive a single mother up the walls are balanced by her contacts with the outside world. With groups such as these she learns skills that will help her sell herself on the employment market when the time comes.

"But I can make money working at home, I am sure I can," a number of women have said to me. Linda, like many other women, loved to sew. She had been making the square dance costumes for herself and her husband while they were members of a local dance group. The other dancers had raved over their cleverness and had hinted that she ought to make some for them. So—wouldn't that be a fine idea? She could bring in an income while staying at home and doing what she liked to do. *Watch it, Linda!*

Well, she told herself, if I am going to make a great number of these costumes and sell them at the local boutique, then wouldn't it be a good idea to buy that expensive, professional sewing machine to speed up my work? I could do so much better with this machine. And then, I could use more work room, so I think I will just bring in a carpenter to build me some counters and shelves and get some better lighting installed here in the old utility room. I don't have to worry about these expenditures because they are all going to be tax deductible!

She arranges for all this to be done, she runs out to the boutique and takes her orders—not very many of them, but she goes home happily to sew on her new equipment in the newly remodeled workroom. She sells a few items, then branches out (not everyone in town, it seems, wants square dance costumes) to include alterations and straight dressmaking. Pressure is on her now to deliver her work, so she hires a neighboring student to run around town and do that . . . and at the end of a few months, she decides it is time to take stock.

Is her business a success? Well, if being very busy is a measure of business success, I guess you would have to say that it is. If making money is the idea, however, the situation is a mess. Adding up all of her costs and subtracting those from the money she is taking in, she has to admit that she is making less than a dollar an hour. Let's face it, the job of working at home and sewing for pay is the luxury of the woman who doesn't really want or need to make money. She must either have a working husband or money from her investments; she will almost never make enough to support herself. The added attraction of the tax deduction should *never* be the reason for doing anything. We are aiming for a profit, not for losses on paper making for interesting deductions. You may tell me "Look— there are exceptions." I am aware of that. If one has an outstanding ability to design, if cheap labor can be hired to help produce that unique invention, it is just possible to make a bona fide business of it. But women so often imagine that they can support themselves sewing at home, and so often fail miserably at it, that I want to warn you specifically about this dream.

Going into Business

There are ways—and there are other ways—of going into business for yourself. Probably the best approach is to begin by working for someone else, learning by watching everything that an experienced person does. This is the old apprentice system, and it still makes a lot of sense. I saw a neighbor of mine, a recent divorcée, get herself into a very nice situation by using this method. Ginger wanted to get herself rolling again but did not need to make a great deal of money right away. In a large shopping center nearby she spotted an ad for help in an attractive shoe store. She was hired at first just to come in a few days a week, but she applied her very good set of brains to learning what that business was all about from A to Z. By the time the owner wanted to sell, a few years later, Ginger was ready to buy. She knew all the suppliers, she understood the market and the bookkeeping system. She knew the individual customers and their preferences. Gradually Ginger had made herself into a pro in this business and she did very well with it.

Jean's story does not have such a happy ending. She got caught in a common business trap you should avoid. Jean had worked in a cooperative day-care center when her children were young and had enjoyed it. She had gone to the local college for courses in child development and had finally obtained a degree so that she was qualified to run a center of her own. How exciting! Now she was divorced; she had arranged to share an apartment with another woman, so she told herself she did not need to make money right away. With a sizable loan from her credit union, she hurried out to buy the day-care center she had had her eye on. It was filled with possibilities—only needed some intelligent, loving care to make it work.

She knew from the beginning exactly how this center ought to look, and Jean began to sink money into it. She took no salary, but invested her own energy and back-breaking labor. Slowly but surely the center began to catch on until at last it *was* a "success." It was bright and attractive; there was a waiting list and she was much admired in the community. Meanwhile, her bank account was in terrible shape and Jean was exhausted. She decided finally that she had done what she set out to do, and she might as well sell the center and move on. After waiting some time for a buyer, she collected pretty nearly her asking price and sat down to do her final figuring. It turned out that, taking everything into consideration on paper, she had just about broken even. She had no profit whatever to show for those years of labor. There were other rewards for her, of course— but this was not a good business transaction. All in all, it had to be regarded as a luxury for Jean.

It is a common failure of the new businesswoman to try to create the *best* nursery school, the best shop or service or whatever, without stopping to understand just how long it will take for that project to turn around and support its owner. Very often the owner is not experienced enough to go slowly in trying to make it "perfect," and she does not realize that she must charge for her own labor and expenditure of energy. She is still thinking in unprofessional terms, not knowing that it may be a considerable time—if ever—before this enterprise will be able to pay back even expenses. Avoid this sort of situation like the plague! Look for courses at your local college or given privately (often by retired business people) to help you with wise financial planning for your enterprise. The Small Business Administration, a federal agency, might also be a source of help. Seek out professional groups involved in the type of service or product you plan to offer. They have been there. They may have a great deal of guidance to offer you.

Going into Partnership

Judy and Josie are going into partnership! Neither has ever been in business before, but they have got it all figured out and they are eager to get started. They have decided that they are going to deal in services. People in their community need all sorts of little jobs done for them, and are willing to pay. "Anything legal that anyone wants done—we will do it. It's as simple as that," they say.

The first thing we need, says Judy, is some good-looking stationery and some business cards. She hurries out to order these from the printer while Josie runs down to the local newspaper to place an ad. Both of them write checks on their personal accounts, and then they sit back and wait. What do you know? They have a call from a neighbor on their very first ad. The visiting mother-in-law needs a ride to the airport. Great! One of the girls picks up the first client and off they go. *What shall I charge?* she wonders. Oh well, let's say five dollars. Now Judy and Josie have a problem. What are they going to do with the profits of this little enterprise? Oh dear, how shall we explain it to them? They haven't got a profit and if they go on this way, it's very unlikely that they ever will. They haven't even got a chauffeur's license, either of them—and they are likely to end up in trouble over that.

Small business people like Judy and Josie are what I call "pass-throughs." They are simply pipelines through which money travels without having any effect on them. They collect fees for their services and then pass those fees on to others in the form of payments for ads, for equipment, for gasoline, for licenses and insurance of various kinds. They run around looking busy but the money never ends up in their own pockets. They failed to get organized.

If you are going into partnership, you don't need to be a corporate lawyer and you don't even necessarily need to hire one. But you do need to draw up some simple papers stating exactly what you are agreeing to. You need to know what your running costs are going to be. You should figure your labor in terms of hourly pay and see whether it is really going to be worth it to you, before you go any farther. A fee schedule should be put into writing, and you should not forget about taxes while you are doing all this.

We hear a lot about deductibles being so helpful the minute you are "in business," but be assured that the IRS will make you prove that you really *are* in business, not just playing at it.

And don't forget that the idea is not to pile up deductibles but to make a worthwhile profit for yourself. If you are going to set up a joint business account with your new partner, place in this account only the amount of money that is actually needed to pay current bills, sharing equally in that deposit. All kinds of things can happen to money that is left lying around in such an account. There should never be a balance higher than necessary until you are much further along in this enterprise. If you are putting in important amounts—and I would call anything over $1,000 important money— have an attorney check over your partnership agreement. And don't forget to check on the attorney's fees before you hire that professional! You certainly don't want to spend your first offerings to the new business entirely on the fees that confirm your agreement.

When you have all this done, keep in mind that

having a lot of customers doesn't make you successful. *Having a profit makes you successful.* Only the figures on paper will tell that story, so make up your mind to keep detailed records from the very beginning. Move ahead one step at a time, and examine your progress in frequent, frank talks with your partner. Your agreement is not written on stone—it can be changed as the necessity arises. The secret of success in small business is to stay alert, to know exactly what you are doing at all times—and why.

Fringe Benefits

We've looked at a good many of the job possibilities for the divorced woman, but don't ignore the possibility of a new phenomenon called "job-sharing." Many companies are setting up their employment schedules these days so that you can work part time at the same job that is taken during the rest of the forty-hour week by another person. In this way you can get the advantages of working part time plus some of the benefits of being in the corporate structure, and those are not to be ignored in your present situation: Social Security, insurance, perhaps entry into a pension plan.

If it's been many years since you have worked on a nine-to-five basis, you may dread it unreasonably. Perhaps your real interests lie in one of the arts—and yet you are smart enough to know that you are not going to be one of those rare poets or painters who will be able to support herself on what she earns with the sale of her art. How do you go about approaching the labor market and the world of industry? Well, a job-sharing situation might be one possible answer for you. Another, looking at the considerable fringe benefits offered by some companies, might be a job in a factory which leaves your mind free to roam most of the time while you perform some fairly automatic and mechanical task. Then, when you leave work at the end of the day, you are going to have some creative energy left to take home with you.

Meantime you may have had a good, solid meal in the company cafeteria so you can heat up a cup of soup for yourself while you do your writing or your painting in the evening. This, in turn, gives you free time that others must spend on shopping for groceries— but you have things to do for yourself that you find more interesting. Your medical insurance, which might be very costly purchased on your own, is usually a part of the company's employment package, so you have that additional security and peace of mind as well.

It seems to me that anyone with extremely powerful outside interests and great creative drive might be able to handle an eight-hour-a-day job as well, for such advantages. I don't know many painters who actually paint forty hours per week. And I am against having my clients shut themselves up in their own homes at any time. I want them to be stimulated by the outside world, challenged at every turn by the people and the events around them. I am very much encouraged by the arrival on the scene of job-sharing possibilities. Yet, if this is not going to be available to you, I would rather see you go after something carefully chosen that would take forty hours a week rather than sit home dreaming your life and your bank account away, to no eventual purpose.

Now I'm the Businesswoman

Claire came to me recently and told me "Hey, I've arrived! I've been asked to join a local businesswoman's club." Claire had been struggling to establish her small boutique and she had been doing very well indeed with it, but she needed all the help she could get. I hated to say anything that might douse her enthusiasm, but I did warn her gently that this might not be the *kind* of woman's club she really wanted. After the first meeting, she came back to see me in a state of confusion and dismay.

"I went there to talk about business, Mary," she said to me. "I wanted to learn something and I wanted to share my own experience. Can you believe that these women sat around making plans for their monthly social function—they meet for lunch every week, it seems—and talking about things we could sew and things we could cook for some picnic? Then they talked about raising money for somebody's scholarship. I was bored nearly out of my mind, and I have wasted my time!"

Yes, I could believe, having been through this sort of thing myself. Unfortunately, most of the weekly men's *or* women's luncheon groups are PR outlets for the companies represented in their membership. The dues and the fees for the luncheon are paid by the employer in an effort to create a good image for his firm. While it is a fine thing, of course, to raise money for scholarships, this is not going to help the business-woman who is serious about developing her own independent career. She needs something quite different from this essentially social gathering.

In time, Claire found what she was looking for. It was the local *business owner's* group—a number of women getting together on quite another basis. These are individuals who are responsible for the success or the failure of their businesses, their investments, and their energy. They do not discuss fund-raising or pot-luck parties. They have solid dues of $100 a year coming from their own pockets and they spend some of that money to send a representative from their group to a management seminar, pay for her time, and expect her to report back to the group. They hire outstanding speakers to help them with continuing education. They are a real support group for one another, and they don't have a great many meetings because they don't have time for them. They have a very loose board arrangement and they keep all the "clubwork" to an absolute minimum.

These, in other words, are serious women who have learned the fundamental lesson I want to pass on to readers of this book when they enter the world beyond the kitchen door. Too many women have a habit of thinking small. They think of money in cookie-jar terms. They underestimate their own energies, their own abilities. They refuse to take themselves seriously. They play at business, rather than work at it. They try to raise money in the small, piddling ways that simply are not going to succeed. I think this is because we have been brainwashed into thinking that we can't succeed, and we don't want to look foolish trying. And therefore we don't try. So we end up cooking a boring casserole for the company picnic instead of marching down to the bank, investing our well-earned profits where they will do us some good. Throw the cookie jar away, ladies! Let's go for the big money now. It's about time.

Chapter 10

THE NEXT MAN: DOING IT DIFFERENTLY

YOU'VE COME THROUGH the worst of the trauma of divorce; now, in all likelihood, you are beginning to heal. Nerves that were battered—nerves you thought would be numb forever— are waking up again and reporting some pleasant sensations. The possibility of happiness seems once more a reality, and you begin to communicate, to enjoy, to accept an invitation here and there. It dawns on you that there may be a person like you out there, someone who would like to begin again, to offer real sharing and honest concern. Can this be true? Yes—when the pain is really gone, when you are less afraid of making the same mistake all over again.

What was the mistake? In the divorces I have observed, the situation was never that simple. Perhaps in personal, human terms there really wasn't a mistake. People simply did what they believed to be right at that particular time in their lives; then they changed, or the circumstances changed. It goes without saying that the more we can learn from the past, the better we can do in the future. Still, there's no point in indulging in lengthy bouts of self-blame and remorse. It's far better to take a careful look at the past and then get yourself up and walk firmly away from it. Don't confuse the emotional mess you are leaving with the hard financial facts. If you have learned something about money management from this book, you are going to keep at least that aspect of your future life in sensible perspective and under your own control. Or so I hope.

What worries me, when I see that new man moving into your life, is that you will throw caution to the winds and begin making financial decisions with your heart instead of your head. *DON'T! STOP! SLOW DOWN!* It's perfectly all right to fall in love—in fact, it's wonderful. But this new relationship, if you are thinking about living together or about marrying, is bound to involve finances. There is no way you can get around this question; it won't go away. At some time there will have to be a discussion about money management. How much will you tell him? What will you dare to expect of him in return? How will you know that he is telling the truth? *Oh, but he is so wonderful, I know he would never lie.* You know no such thing. Have you forgotten the con artist on the vestry of the local church so soon?

No Strings?

All right, you have found someone who may be that very right person for you. Things are moving along fairly rapidly, and by now the two of you can hardly bear to be apart. Wouldn't it be easier, ever so much more pleasant, if you moved in together? Cheaper, too. No sense both of you paying rent on two separate apartments—or being tied up with two separate mortgages. Or is there?

Thinking back over your previous marriage, you may very well decide that you want "no strings" this time, at least at first. You have been burned, and you want to go into this cautiously. You'll test the new situation before making that ultimate commitment. At the same time, you may have had times of bitterness over money during that marriage. The very thought of bringing the subject up makes you feel fearful about the possibility of losing your new friend. It could be painful, of course. And yet, this is something you are simply going to have to do. Money is as much of an everyday reality as love, and if you don't deal with it directly, it is going to turn around and punish you.

What is the right time for plunging into such a discussion? I would say that when the idea of cohabitation becomes at all serious you must look at the economic realities together *before* making any further moves. Who is going to pay the rent? Who is going to pay for the groceries? What about telephone? Utilities? What is going to happen to the empty house or apartment one of you is leaving? There is no such thing as a live-together relationship between people who are emotionally involved without strings.

Look at it this way. If saving money really were the motive for the two of you to move in together, you would have done better to invite a friend. Everything would have been relatively simple then—each to his or her own life, own occupations, own bed. All bills for food, shelter, and utilities neatly divided down the middle. But be truthful with yourself. This is not what you are doing when you set up housekeeping with that fascinating and bewitching man! What you are doing with him is setting up a pretend domestic scene, a quasi-marriage.

If that's what you really want to do, okay. But be aware of the fact that you are in a dangerous situation emotionally and financially, and don't kid yourself. Draw up a written statement of your financial expectations. If large sums are involved, you may need an attorney to help you put it into legal language; ask professional advice about making this a legally binding agreement. It doesn't have to be anything elaborate. There are no standard forms to fill out on this kind of relationship; it depends upon your own personal wishes and needs. Your statement can be as simple or as complicated as your financial reality demands.

The Quasi-Marriage: Remaining Responsible

Traditional marriage involves mutual work toward mutual financial goals. Not so the quasi-marriage. So protect yourself in various ways if you are entering into this kind of relationship.

First and foremost: let *nothing* persuade you to invade the capital which we have called your Old Age Pension. (I will give you the same advice again later in this chapter, when we will be discussing the possibilities of another marriage.) It cannot be said too often that this is your main position of financial safety—and perhaps your only one, if you are in a quasi-marital situation. Make up your mind that if this new relationship requires you to dig into your capital for any reason, then it is not for you.

Second: never, never, set up joint checking accounts or joint savings accounts with your partner in a quasi-marriage situation. Never make major purchases such as a car or a set of expensive furniture jointly with him. Face the fact that this is a temporary relationship as it now exists. It may change, yes. But right now you are living with it from month to month, and you must be able to pick up your clothes and move, or see your partner do just that, without financial entanglement.

Third: keep your own home base available if you possibly can, either the place you own or the place you rent, if you decide to move in with him. Rent or sublet if necessary, but don't throw yourself into a situation where you will find yourself homeless if an emotional arrangement doesn't work out. This may sound like a very obvious precaution to take, but I have seen women take this chance again and again when they are infatuated and the results have too often been deeply damaging. The loss of a home can be like the loss of a limb, to a woman. In a rising real estate market it can also be a financial catastrophe.

Now, you may very well decide to share the rent and the utilities on a fifty-fifty basis. Fine. I see nothing wrong with that, provided there are no other joint expenses undertaken. What if Harry has twice as much income as Rhoda? Should she pay half their entertainment costs even if he has a lovely expense account? These are the items that must come up for frank discussion ahead of time and be listed on paper where you can both look at them. You both know the arrangement can be reworked if the financial situation or the emotional situation should change. You both know, in the meantime, exactly what is expected of you. You are not supporting this man, and he is not supporting you.

Wifey

In another sort of arrangement, he may actually be supporting you. You may be playing house in a rather old-fashioned way, doing all those wifey things for him in exchange for your living expenses. "Making nice" as an occupation, without benefit of marriage contract. If this is something you enjoy doing, I am not going to argue with you, I am just going to ask you to face facts. Again, be aware that this is a purely temporary arrangement. When and if it ends, it is very likely that you will have absolutely nothing to claim for all your work. If you have given up a career (as in the famous Marvin case) you may have lost professional advancement on the gamble that this would be a permanent commitment; you may or may not be able to recover a dime. Laws about common-law marital commitments differ in various states; if you enter into a long-term relationship of this kind, it will be your responsibility to look up the law in your area and know exactly what you are getting into. Don't wait for the men to check this out just because they have usually taken control of the finances involved. Act like a grown-up and do it yourself.

Luxury Item

Lately I have had a few women tell me that they are perfectly willing to support their men as long as these partners of theirs in quasi-marriage continue to offer love and companionship. This is an interesting new twist on an old financial arrangement, and I am always curious to meet such men; at times, I must admit, they are quite charming. Fine, I tell these women, as long as you know exactly what you are buying and as long as you are sure that you can really afford it. Make sure you understand that this man is not really a partner or even a necessity—he is a luxury item.

The Realistic Couple

There are couples who make quite a good thing, I believe, out of the quasi-marriage situation. Often these are older people, perhaps retired, who want not only the sharing of rent and the sharing of space, but personal commitment as well. Tax laws tending to give rise to such situations are showing signs of change, at last; no longer will it be such a financial hardship for such couples to marry if that is what they wish to do. Some, for other reasons perhaps, will still prefer a less formal arrangement.

Gertrude and Harry, for example, are living together very happily now in a bungalow in a sunny, suburban location. They are not young and foolish, and they have been able to come to grips with all of the ambiguities in their situation. Together they live better than they could separately, on two small retirement incomes; each knows that his and her own children will inherit anything left when the time comes, for they have made careful wills to that effect. Over the years, the relationship between these two has grown gradually. They did not rush into anything. They discussed every financial issue as it arose and worked out a flexible series of compromises. They did not let disagreements about money build up, then flare up into major arguments. At every step of the way, Gertrude has guarded her own Old Age Pension—made up partly of her savings of many years, partly from her Individual Retirement Account, partly from a small settlement of property from her divorce many years ago. She has this money well invested. Why then don't they marry—and what is the difference here between quasi-marriage and the real thing?

Actually, I think they may marry eventually. Until now, for a number of purely personal reasons, they have not wanted to. The difference between this sort of arrangement and marriage is not tremendous, but the financial realities are apt to be different in some ways worth thinking about. Gertrude has made a decision not to build up a commonly held set of properties, even though she knows that 85 percent of women end up alone. Chances are overwhelmingly large that she will not have the double income to help her out in her latter years. She is willing to risk the possibility that this relationship may end at any time, and so is Harry. I don't say that this would be a comfortable situation for a great many people, but I won't criticize this couple; they have been entirely honest with one another, they know exactly what they are doing.

She Married Prince Charming

Marriage, in fact, is not always the financial answer—even when the man you marry is tremendously rich. Where did we ever get the idea (out of the old dime novels, I suppose) that the little girl who married Prince Charming was going to be happy—and also decked with diamonds—for the rest of her life? What if you do find a wealthy man and the two of you decide to marry? Just how great is that going to be?

I recall the day Rosalind, forty-five, came to me after about ten years of marriage to her PC. She had a sense that the marriage was about to dissolve, and she wanted to know what was in store for her, just in case. Philip had a large income from an old family trust fund, and they had been living very comfortably on that. There was absolutely nothing in this marriage that could be called community property, so there was nothing to divide. Rosalind had lived in Philip's house, and that had been paid for out of separate funds. Nothing in the house had been purchased during their time together. They had not accumulated any savings. There had been no gifts, no prenuptial agreement. Everything was his. Nothing was hers. Could she go to court and demand payment at least for her services as a housewife? She could try, but chances were that the law would ignore that. If he had been untrue or had physically harmed her, a state or two might consider giving her a settlement on those grounds; but today, when the no-fault divorce is generally the rule, one is rarely able to seek damages.

Could Rosalind seek spousal support? Even this might be hard to obtain, for she had been a secretary before her marriage and had done some temporary work for friends while Philip was traveling alone during the marriage. Clearly, she was able to support herself. She would not have the standard of living she had been accustomed to, but she would not be on welfare either, and the latter consideration is of primary importance to the court.

Can we lay the blame for such a situation on Prince Charming? Not altogether, certainly. Men who live on "old money" are apt to be in the toils of the prestigious old law firm whose purpose is to guard that ancient hoard. Usually they will not permit the scion of a fortune to express whatever generosity he might feel. Rosalind was at fault for going naïvely into this situation without setting up any safeguards for herself. She should have had a prenuptial arrangement naming her as co-owner of their house or co-owner of some definite amount of property. She should have thought of this marriage as a business venture for both partners to work at, so that something solid was going to be built up in both their names. Any woman who marries money, or marries in a situation where the money is her own, without proper legal agreement is asking for trouble.

The story of Rosalind is a sad one, but not nearly so sad as the one I hear even more often. A divorced woman has been left a nice little settlement, let's say. She lives for a time very carefully on the income from that plus temporary alimony and salary from a part-time job. Gloria is over fifty-five and she feels safe in coasting along, looking forward to her "retirement" in ten years or so. She has never worked outside the home before and she does not intend to make a full-time career for herself now. When her spousal support stops, she begins dipping into her capital, not realizing that her retirement money is not going to be nearly enough to support her, not realizing that she is likely to be very much alive and hungry at the age of eighty-five.

Still, she feels uneasy about her situation. When an utterly delightful man comes along and offers to marry her, she is thrilled to hear him say that he will help her manage her money for the rest of her life. She will have total security with him! Gloria falls head over heels in love. No more worries. She has found the perfect companion at last. Gloria remarries, and then her trouble really begins.

Her new husband goes off to work every day, but he never seems to have any money in the bank when it is time to pay bills. She dips into her capital again, not wanting to quarrel with him over anything so mundane as finances. After all, he has promised to manage everything nicely for her—he has just been too busy lately, and he must be suffering like everyone else from the inroads of inflation. Pretty soon they need a new car. Charles says he is having cash-flow problems at his firm. Would she please just pay for the car on a temporary basis, and he will pay her back as soon as things improve a little? Gloria pays for the car, but when she asks very gently to have her money back at the end of that year, Charles shouts at her and goes storming out of the house. Gloria's capital is being very rapidly depleted now, and suddenly Charles does not seem to be so fond of her any more. "Can this be happening to me?" Gloria wonders. "I have already had one divorce; I can't bear to go through another one." She decides that it is all her fault. She goes to a pyschiatrist. She gets a new hairdo and buys expensive clothes— with her own money, of course. By now she has learned that Charles becomes abusive or vanishes every time she mentions the fact that she needs his financial cooperation. Her self-esteem is lower and lower. Finally she decides on a romantic little holiday for just the two of them, as a gamble with the last of her money. Charles goes along, but he is oddly distracted. Charles is thinking about the rich young widow down the street. When they get home, Charles departs, and Gloria is left with the rest of the bills, a new divorce, and a financial catastrophe on her hands.

Can you believe that any woman could be so simple? Well, I have seen variations of this story over, and over, and over again. The Glorias of this world are loving and giving individuals who simply don't have the gumption to insist on their rights. Because they are women, they think they should offer everything they have to their men (that is the traditional, sacrificial feminine way, isn't it?) and it doesn't occur to them to ask for anything legally or financially solid in return. They confuse an emotional position with an economic one and end by cooperating in their own financial collapse.

I mention this particularly in connection with the divorced woman who has received a solid settlement, because I see it happening so very often here. Cynical men flock around the naïve divorcée, waiting for handouts these days as they once were found preying on the inheritance of the innocent widow. Don't be naïve! Don't be innocent! Come hell or high water *or another man,* hang onto the settlement intact, and remember at all times that it is your Old Age Pension. You were awarded it by the court, but what if you had worked for every penny of it doing laundry or on your feet selling at your local department store? Would you be so careless with your earnings in a situation like that? You have just as much right to that settlement as you would if you had earned it. You got it because the law said you should have it. *Don't give it away.*

Previous Commitments

Betsey fell in love with an older man, but he was exciting. So many of them are! They were going to be married soon, and she came to me for advice. The problem was that he had four kids and was still supporting three of them; he also had a commitment to pay spousal support to his ex-wife. This was all right with Betsey—

she was no baby. Divorced from her first, puppy love, she was in her early thirties and knew a thing or two. What bothered her was the possibility that they might never be able to afford a child of their own. She was willing to help Joe with his obligations even if it meant that she had to keep working indefinitely, but she didn't want to miss the entire experience of motherhood.

I don't usually mince words, and I didn't with Betsey. I told her this might be the price she would have to pay for marrying the man. You marry a man and you share his life. You share his life and you share his obligations. I told her to look upon that as a reality and make up her mind—not to cry "unfair" later.

Possibly, I told her, you two could set aside some of your income on a regular basis. You could hold down your standard of living so as to build a little savings account in both your names. In time, you could take a year off from work and get that family of yours started. But remember, I told her, that this plan will work only if it is clearly agreed on, if it is acceptable to both of you.

Be My Guest—Be My Curator

In all the years I have been listening to stories about women and money, I have never found a surer setup for failure than the Next Marriage that starts in the ex-wife's (or the deceased wife's) home. In some cases the husband really wants a sort of permanent guest. He does not want a real wife who will move the furniture around, or even perhaps put it all into storage and bring in her own things. In other situations it is obvious that he is really living in a museum; if it was a divorce, this may be a place full of angry and jealous memories. He wants the new wife to be curator of this museum, in charge of the dusting and polishing. Physically, he's not ready to move—emotionally, he's not either. In these circumstances, don't marry him! Insist that you start out fresh with a real home that is new to both of you.

Yes, it will involve some expense to make such a move, but it will be worth it. Don't sell the old house. Get out of it and rent it. Hold onto that property while you give the new situation a long, thorough test. I would advise the same thing if you were tempted to move your new mate into the house you shared with someone else in a previous marriage. Move to an exciting new situation together—something you can fully share. But don't burn your bridges behind you. Get that house of yours rented, and wait a while. Yes, someone may come along and mess it up. So be it! Much better to spend some more money cleaning it up than to find sometime down the road that you want it back terribly—and now it is too late. You must not lose your Old Age Pension, you see, and you mustn't lose your home, above all things, in the excitement of a new relationship. Shelter and sustenance are things you are always going to need.

And now, having mentioned all sorts of potential difficulties in relation to the New Man in Your Life, I must say that these *can* be the happiest situations of all. People who have lived and suffered are apt to be a great deal wiser than those who are just starting out with a head full of dreams and stars in their eyes.

Women are wonderfully flexible in this way. Sometimes women really amaze me. Again and again I see them pick themselves up off the floor after terrible marriages and utterly crushing divorce experiences. Then I see them go on, more determined than ever to find satisfaction, independence, and happiness. I see them learning to live on their own and, time and again, daring to love once more.

I have scolded and I have pushed you this way and that, not always calling you very nice names, in the course of this book. But never forget that, although we live in an affluent society these days, when we talk about "old, alone, and poor" we are still talking about women. Husbands and fathers are not going to be there any more, as a general rule, to support us. We live longer than our men, anyway. Too many women find, in our times, that they have outlived their money. I have wanted better than that for you. And I will go on shouting, if necessary, to help you get it.

This book, in other words, has been written with a deep sense of caring for all women. I am willing to face the fact along with you that the financial life of women is still a very emotional issue. In the past, the average woman had very few choices. She was bound to her husband by her very real economic needs, and there were few ways in which she could possibly provide for herself. The fact that we are now in a time of transition is often frightening, always challenging; we feel bewildered that the financial roles of men and of women are no longer clearly defined.

Are we ready at last to put away the classic storybook notion of Ideal Marriage? I doubt that there were many couples at any time in our history who could fit that picture.

Today women are becoming motivated to be self-supporting. We know now that our only purpose on earth is *not* to be bearers of children. We have a choice, now. Few women will ever again accept the role of being purely dependent. We want to be equal partners in marriage.

I profoundly believe that this new, equal relationship will serve to remove a great many unfair burdens that have been place, up until now, upon men. In writing about divorce as a financial transaction I have aimed to show women their full responsibility as adults in one of the most difficult and trying situations they will ever face. I hope that in looking at divorce in this way we can also remember to see the responsibility of marriage somewhat differently. With this new equality, there should be a growth of new respect. We should understand that in every marriage from now on, both partners must share full responsibility as equal adults— for earning, for parenting, for companionship, for everlasting love and concern.

INDEX